This book is dedicated in loving memory and honor of my cousin
and godchild, Lauren Cecil,
who was suddenly called to Heaven in July 2013.

Lauren,

Your bright, innocent eyes and that contagious smile

Conveyed a love most precious and pure.

You were only here for a little while,

Yet you have changed me forevermore.

I will *always* love you!

Love, "Aunt" Mandy

I too will have my say;
I too will tell what I know.
For I am full of words,
and the spirit within me compels me;

Job 32:17-18

WISDOM from WILBUR

How My DOG Has Brought Me Closer to GOD

Mandy Lawrence

CONTENTS

PROLOGUE: IN THE BEGINNING

For as long as I can remember, dogs have brought much joy to my life. My mother often tells the story of my first encounter with a dog. I was about six months old, and my family was gathered in my grandparents' yard enjoying a nice, sunny day. Mama remembers having me propped on her hip when a dog showed up by her side, and when I saw its face looking up at me, I just burst into laughter. Supposedly, this was the first time I had ever laughed uncontrollably—to the point I could barely catch a breath. My family recalls that they were all laughing hysterically because I was laughing, or actually cackling, they say! Since I have no recollection of this incident, I can honestly say that I have loved dogs before I can even remember.

Many of my earliest memories include dogs. I have a few memories of the dachshund, Casey, that my parents got before I was born. But since he ran away when I was only three years old, my memories of him are rather vague. I have no recollection of the Bassett Hound, Molly, that my parents got after Casey disappeared, although I've come across a few pictures of me with her. Supposedly, Molly wasn't with us very long; she had a bad habit of wandering off and frequently stirred up trouble in some of our neighbors' yards, so my parents gave her away. The next dog my parents got was an Irish setter named Megan, and the only reason I remember her at all is because she terrified me!

She always jumped on me and knocked me to the ground, leaving me nearly breathless and with dirt and tears streaming down my face. I think this is why my parents ended up giving her away after only a short while, too.

My "real" memories began around the time I was four years old when we welcomed Heidi, a precious dachshund puppy, into our home and family. I was an only child, so she quickly became my best buddy. I always looked forward to watching her run like lightning—with her long ears flopping—across the 100-yard field to our house every evening as my mom and I drove down our gravel road. Heidi would spend the day getting spoiled at my great uncle and aunt's house (our neighbors) when we weren't home, but she would always come running back to our house the moment she spotted our vehicle coming down the drive! I was pretty heart-broken when she died as the result of a wild animal attack one night outside of our rural North Carolina home. Her death was the first memorable experience I had with death and loss, so this was a rather difficult time for me. I remember thinking of Heidi and crying every time "Somewhere Out There" (a popular song sung by Linda Ronstadt and James Ingram) played on the radio.

Thankfully, though, it wasn't long after Heidi died that my mom and dad took me to pick out a new dachshund puppy for Christmas. I was only six at the time, but I vividly remember the joy I felt as I held my new puppy in the back seat on the long drive home that cold, rainy night. After looking through a list of names included in our old dictionary, I decided to name my new best friend Bridgett Kisses. Bridgett quickly became my little baby—I still have pictures of me pushing her in my doll stroller!

Not long after Bridgett turned two, she gave birth for the first and only time. My parents had planned to make some extra money from this Christmas litter, but their plans were spoiled when Bridgett's litter turned out to be a single puppy! I remember not being able to sleep a wink the snowy November night that Bridgett became a mom. My parents and I had returned home from an outing to find Bridgett in the early stages of labor, and Mama made me go straight to bed as she made plans to assist with the delivery. When the sun *finally* came up the next morning, I rushed to the laundry room to meet the new, precious addition to our family—later named Abigail Little Kisses. As you can imagine, Bridgett and Abby were my pride and joy during my childhood years. I developed a very close bond with them since they were my only "siblings."

God surely knew what He was doing by waiting to take my Bridgett away the summer after I finished nursing school … I honestly might have been too fragile and grief-stricken to graduate if she had died before then. Her death hit me very hard. I remember frequently becoming nauseated from the deep sadness I felt after she died. When she came home with us, I was a six-year-old little girl playing with dolls; when she died, I was a 22-year-old young woman on the brink of starting my adult life. I still had Abby for a while longer; she died two years later at nearly 16 years of age. I still get emotional sometimes when I think of Bridgett and Abby, especially when I come across pictures of them. They are a part of so many of my cherished memories, and I will forever be grateful for the chance to love and be loved by them.

In 2002, a little more than a year after Bridgett died, I moved out of my childhood home. Not long after that, I received a wonderful Christmas gift—a dachshund puppy I named Winnie. She nearly destroyed my house during her early puppy stage, but she was a sweet, loyal companion who brought me much comfort during a difficult time in my life. However, those difficulties led to some major changes—changes which made it impractical for me to keep Winnie. So, fortunately, her "Papaw" (my dad) gladly adopted her. This was obviously God's plan because Winnie has been one of my dad's closest companions for many years, and I still get to enjoy being around her from time to time as well.

Along Came Wilbur

For several years, I went without the companionship of a dog to call my own. In 2004, God blessed me with a wonderful husband, Shane, who is a travel agent. As soon as we got married, we began traveling as much as our work schedules would allow. Since most places are trying to "sell" my husband on promoting their resort or hotel, we get to stay at many wonderful destinations for an ultra-discounted rate and often for free. Also, we're usually treated like royalty when we go somewhere; more times than not, we walk into luxurious rooms or suites and find champagne, chocolate-covered strawberries, and other gifts awaiting us.

Having all these great, free getaways is definitely a blessing; however, when you are an animal-lover like me, the situation becomes a little complicated. Although I always wanted a dog, I knew it would be impractical for us to have one since we were on the go so much. So for the first few years of our marriage, I just loved on the neighborhood dogs and enjoyed the time I could spend with Winnie (the dog my dad "adopted" from me).

During this time, I also made frequent visits to the pet store at the mall, dragging my husband along, of course—I'm sure the employees got tired of seeing us walk in, asking to take one of the puppies back to the play area. These visits usually satisfied my need to snuggle and play with a furry friend; that is, until one of the visits ended with me in tears. On that particular occasion, I quickly bonded with a little black and tan dachshund puppy, and I wanted him desperately! I even named him, calling him "Cookie" because his little paws—tan with black spots—looked exactly like chocolate chip cookies. Although in the past I hadn't much cared for the black and tan dachshunds (being partial to brown, female ones), this little cookie stole my heart. I begged my husband to let me take him home, even though they were asking $1,000 for him! Since I'm normally rather thrifty, I knew I was smitten when I was ready to hand over three times the amount of money I could pay for another puppy just like him.

My husband, being rational and not nearly the dog-lover I was, put his foot down and practically dragged me out of the pet store that day. I may not have been successful in convincing him to buy little "Cookie," but after this ordeal, he was convinced that we needed a dog. He said he wanted to see me smile and light up more often—the way he saw me do when I was around dogs. So even though we knew it would mean having more responsibilities in our lives than we were used to, we finally decided to just go for it.

After searching online for local dachshund puppies, my husband and I decided to get one from a breeder located about an hour from our hometown. I doubt I'll ever forget that cool October evening when we went to pick out our puppy. Upon arrival at the breeder's home, we walked up to a small fenced-in area in the garage and saw five dachshund puppies bouncing around. We had initially decided to pick the runt of the litter because we wanted a tiny dog, but there was just something drawing me to one of the other pups. The breeder then pointed at that particular one and said, "This one never stops wagging his tail!" One look at his precious face, his adorable chocolate chip cookie-paws, and that little wagging tail, and my mind was made up!

On the way home that evening, my heart was full of love as I snuggled my new little baby beneath my chin. We were discussing possible names for him when my husband asked, "What was the name of that pig in *Charlotte's Web*?" At this, my eyes lit up, and I instantly knew the perfect name for him .... "Wilbur!" I exclaimed. Since I've always had a thing for pigs, there couldn't have been a more perfect name in my opinion—so Wilbur Waggles it was!

It didn't take long for me to fall head-over-heels for this new addition to our family. Wilbur was a tiny thing, but he had a huge overflow of personality and love, wagging his little tail more than any dog I'd ever seen! Wilbur quickly stole my husband's heart as well, even though he had never been a big dog-lover like me.

Wilbur is now six years old—my, how the time has flown! Adding him to our family was surely the best thing my husband and I ever did.

He stands only inches from the ground and weighs a mere 17 pounds on his chunkiest days, but he's made a giant impact on our lives. Wilbur has brought an immeasurable amount of love, joy, and laughter into our hearts and home. He has taught me a lot, too, especially about my faith. My relationship with Wilbur has given me deeper insights into the nature of God, strengthening the relationship I have with my Heavenly Father.

These insights are what I want to share with you in this book. While I have included some cute stories about Wilbur, most of the content is rather deep—just so you know. I have always felt a calling on my life to share God's message of love and hope with others. In recent years, I believe God has led me down the path of writing this book as a means to fulfill that calling. My prayer for each of you is that through the stories and analogies I share, your love and understanding of God will increase and that you'll gain a deeper realization of the love He has for you as well.

CHAPTER 1: TOUGH LOVE

Wilbur watches me like a hawk as I get his doggie crate down from the closet shelf. His eyes grow wide with anticipation as he realizes he's about to take a little trip. I imagine he's thinking, *Where to?* I load him up in the car and try to get the air vents blowing in his direction since it's approaching 100 degrees outside. Feelings of guilt and anxiety begin to creep in as I think about what I'm about to put my poor Wilbur through.

I soon pull into the parking lot of Jordan Veterinary Hospital and wonder if Wilbur has figured out what's going on yet. I open the car door and see him taking whiffs of the air outside the vet clinic—air saturated with the scent of many other patients. Now I'm sure he knows where we are, and I wonder what he's thinking … Is he nervous or upset? Does he remember what happened to him the last time he was here?

A few minutes later, the vet's assistant is holding Wilbur down on the cold, metal exam table. He looks at me with fearful, questioning eyes, and my heart breaks when I see the doctor walk in with a shot in his hand. I can barely look as the needle goes into Wilbur, but when I do, his eyes appear to be screaming, *Don't you see me here, Mommy?!? Why are you allowing this to happen to me? Why don't you rescue me, Mommy?!?*

At times like these, I wish so badly that dogs could truly understand us. I've been around enough dogs to know that they are very smart animals, and Wilbur's intelligence has actually surprised me on numerous occasions. In fact, I often find myself spelling out words to my husband in order to slide things by him ... If I don't spell out "c-a-r-r-o-t" or "w-a-l-k," Wilbur will take off like a missile to the refrigerator or to the door in eager anticipation. He definitely understands his favorite words! But as a canine, of course, there's only so much he can truly understand.

It saddens and frustrates me that Wilbur will never truly realize why I take him to the vet to be tortured by needles and foreign objects going in places they shouldn't; nor is he ever going to understand why I hold him against his will to brush his teeth (or that I probably hate doing it as much as he despises having it done!). And I know Wilbur will never appreciate me taking a rawhide bone away from him once it's become a choking hazard. I'm sure he probably feels like I'm robbing him when I do this, but I've seen what happens when I don't intervene—I've watched him nearly choke to death on a well-chewed bone and have had to stick my fingers halfway down his throat to clear his airway!

When I think of what some of these scenarios must appear to be in Wilbur's mind, it's hard not to feel guilty. I worry that he thinks I'm punishing or betraying him, and I wish so badly that he could know the rationale behind each thing I do to take care of him. But even though I know he doesn't understand these situations, I am always confident that I'm doing the right thing. While it's hard to watch, I have no doubt that I'm making the right decision in allowing the vet to "torture" him so he can be healthy and live a better, longer life. I know it's better for him to suffer the temporary sting of a needle than to suffer from the disease the immunization is designed to prevent. Likewise, it's better for me to take his bone away than for him to choke on one of the small pieces. I think you see where I'm headed with this point, and whether you are a fellow pet owner or a parent, I imagine you've felt the same way in similar situations.

One day it occurred to me that this overseeing love I demonstrate toward Wilbur likely resembles the type of love God has for me. Just as I would love to make Wilbur understand that I'm doing things he dislikes purely out of love for him, I'm sure God wants me to realize that He allows certain uncomfortable things in my life only out of love for me. And just as it bothers me when I know Wilbur misinterprets my love as harm, it probably grieves God when I don't have faith that He's on my side and has only the best intentions for allowing me to go through painful circumstances.

Have you ever found yourself on the examination table asking God, *Why?* Maybe you've lost a loved one in a tragedy and found yourself angry with God, wondering how He could've allowed something like that to happen. Perhaps you have never endured anything tragic by most people's standards, but you seem to have so many obstacles in your path and can't make sense of your life. Maybe you find yourself repeatedly asking the same question: *Why?* We never completely outgrow that, do we? Like a child who constantly asks for an explanation, we often get fixated on the question, *Why?* I believe our spiritual growth is often hindered because we dwell on the questions instead of moving ahead and trusting that God knows what He's doing. I can certainly relate.

Blessings in Disguise

During my junior year of high school, I started dating a young man and fell head-over-heels in love. We dated for six years, and over this period of time, I often sensed that he wasn't the man God had chosen for me. Unfortunately, my will was stronger than my faith in God's plan. I wanted to be with this man so badly that I pushed all the warnings aside and refused to let him go, and we ended up getting married when we were 23 years old. Our marriage wasn't at all what I had hoped it would be; a little more than a year after our wedding, he went on a business trip to Wales and, in short, never returned.

As you can imagine, I was initially devastated. I had absolutely no idea where my life was headed. My ex-husband later apologized and expressed regrets; he even asked me to move to Europe to be with him. But by that time, I had lost all faith in him and knew that unless he agreed to come back home and attend marriage counseling (which he wouldn't do), our relationship was over. So we divorced about a year later.

I spent a fair share of the days that followed in bed, sinking under a heavy blanket of depression … I had some pretty big pity parties! Fortunately, I also grew closer than ever to God during this difficult period in my life. I developed a passion for reading Christian books, and I remember being inspired and revived by many of them, including Rick Warren's *The Purpose Driven Life*. This book really lit a spark in my soul and helped me put things into perspective. For the first time, I really understood that I was put on this earth for God's glory and purposes—not my own. I tried my best to cling to the promise of God in Jeremiah 29:11, which states:

> "For I know the plans I have for you," declares the
> Lord, "plans to prosper you and not to harm you, plans
> to give you hope and a future."

I still had moments of doubt and loneliness, and I still questioned God. But I held on tight and somehow managed to keep my head above water (thanks to God sustaining me). Then, before I knew it, God put me in the right place at the right time to meet my current husband, Shane. It was under such random circumstances that I knew it had been orchestrated by God alone, especially since our very first conversation began with my husband admiring the cross pendant I was wearing.

What a surprise this was! It was amazing how Shane and I instantly connected and knew we were meant to be together. We've been married for nine years now, and I love him so much. He loves me with all his heart and treats me like a princess (most of the time, anyway). I am so blessed to have a husband who shares my faith, who is fun and outgoing, who respects me more than I even deserve, and who works very hard to provide for me and enable me to fulfill my dreams. Our marriage has had some hard times like any other, but God has certainly blessed me in spite of the broken road I've traveled.

If it weren't for the pain God allowed me to experience with the failure of my first marriage, I don't think I could truly understand or appreciate the blessings I have now. In hindsight, I can see that God always had things under control, even when I felt like my world was turned upside down. God knew every little piece of the puzzle of my life—where each piece had been scattered and exactly how and when to place them back together again. He allowed me to suffer for a time, but it was all worth it to have gained the wonderful blessings He had waiting for me on the other side. I bet you can also identify some times in your life when God allowed you to experience pain (physical and/or emotional) in order to protect you from something worse down the road or to bless you more fully in the future.

Unfortunately, just as Wilbur can't understand my efforts to protect him, we can't always understand God's ways of watching over us. After seeing the connection between my relationship with God in light of my relationship with Wilbur, I can grasp how there are some disappointments that God *has* to allow in my life in order to truly love and protect me.

———

The Good Outweighs the Bad

Many people don't believe in God because there's so much suffering in the world. They argue that a good God wouldn't allow such pain. I can't help but wonder how these people would respond to this statement:

> *By allowing your pets or children to suffer through vaccinations, the pain from a necessary surgical procedure, and/or a spanking for the sake of discipline, you don't love them. If you loved them, you wouldn't have allowed them to suffer.*

Certainly, this statement is irrational. Just because we love someone doesn't mean we shelter them from any and every pain. Ironically, the opposite is true … We allow them to endure a certain amount of hurt and pain *because* we love them.

It's possible that this side of Heaven, we won't see the good that comes from all of our trials and struggles. However, as Christians, we can be assured that there is an eternity of blessings waiting for us on the other side. One of my favorite Scriptures is Romans 8:18, which says:

> For I consider that the sufferings of this present time
> are not worthy *to be compared* with the glory which
> shall be revealed in us (NKJV).

Isn't it encouraging to know that God can see the end result of all our pains, heartaches, and losses? Aren't you heartened by His assurance that our rewards are so great that they aren't even worth comparing to the temporary discomforts we experience in the here and now? Knowing and believing these truths has made all the difference in my life. When I'm about to break, I can close my eyes and know that there is coming a day when I can look back at all the obstacles in my life and consider them insignificant in light of my eternal blessings. Thanks to God's grace, I'm now able to view the painful things that come into my life as essential stepping stones that will lead me to the blessings He has waiting for me.

I hope you realize and choose to believe that God is always looking out for you, too, even when it may not feel that way. Perhaps you're at a place in your life right now where you are doubting God. Unfortunately, I think we've all been there. I understand how scary and uncomfortable it is to be sitting on that exam table with a million questions going through your head, and I know how heartbreaking and discouraging it is to watch a relationship with someone you love fall apart. However, in the midst of difficult situations, it's essential for us to be strong in our faith in God and His sovereignty; we need to trust that He always knows best.

I pray that the example I shared from my life and the analogy regarding Wilbur have better illustrated God's "tough love." Remember that when absolutely *nothing* makes sense to you, *everything* makes perfect sense to God. If you love Him, He is working ALL things out for your eventual good (Romans 8:28). God knows we won't always understand things; He knows that sometimes we will mistakenly perceive His benevolence as harm. In those times, however, we must realize that our Master will stand firm in allowing us to go through certain trials so that He can later reveal to us the depth of His love, protection, and blessings.

CHAPTER 2: HIERARCHY OF KNOWLEDGE

If someone told you that you had to teach a dog to do your job, what approach would you take? Would you simply lecture, or would you use a visual aid like PowerPoint to enhance his understanding? This is silly, right?!? Obviously, any approach you took would be a complete waste of your time and breath. I could talk from now until eternity, yet Wilbur would never be a bit wiser in understanding my perspective and life in the human realm.

As I discussed in the previous chapter, being able to see how much more knowledge I have than Wilbur has given me insight into how God may associate with me and His children. Isaiah 55:8-9 states:

> "For my thoughts are not your thoughts, neither are your ways my ways," declares the LORD. "As the heavens are higher than the earth, so are my ways higher than your ways and my thoughts than your thoughts."

Through this Scripture, I believe God is spelling out rather simply that we cannot understand His thoughts and ways because we humans are in an entirely different ballpark than He is when it comes to knowledge ... just as dogs and humans are.

If you're anything like me, it doesn't take much investigation of God's miraculous craftsmanship to feel extremely in awe of the Creator. Whether I am looking up at the moon and stars or learning about the many complexities of the human body, I feel completely inadequate when comparing my knowledge and abilities with God's. However, it goes against human nature to think of ourselves as being inferior, even when comparing ourselves with God. I can't help but believe this is why so many people do not *allow* themselves to believe in God ... They let pride stand in their way. God makes their knowledge and significance seem like a grain of sand, and perhaps they can't deal with such a strong sense of inferiority.

Unequal Playing Fields

Our society seems to value specialized knowledge more and more. The complex things some people are able to do amaze me. Technology has advanced rapidly in recent years, and there are now experts and specialists in fields we couldn't even imagine 100 years ago. Although there are many people in our world today who perform jobs that have been around for centuries, some exceptionally intelligent people among us build rockets, perform surgery using robotic devices, and develop intricate computer programs. Such people stand apart from the crowd, so to speak, because they possess more knowledge than the average human does.

Similarly, in the canine world, there are certain breeds that stand out as well. Some dogs are known for their great herding skills. Others are known for being great protectors. And some breeds, such as the Border collie, are considered to be more intelligent than others. But when it comes to understanding the human world, dogs are all in the same boat. In other words, even the smartest Border collie alive cannot explain the complexities of being a human to another dog because at the end of the day, they are both still dogs … and we all know that humans and dogs simply "speak" different languages that can never be completely bridged. Do you see where I'm going with this?

I get so irritated when I see television shows that feature rather arrogant scientists talking about evolution and the Big Bang theory as if they are common facts. Since there are still many unanswered questions among us, I can't help but wonder how these scientists are so confident that they (or even the most intelligent person who has ever lived) are qualified and capable of explaining the age-old mysteries of creation and the universe to the rest of us. Every rational person accepts that there are varying degrees of intelligence within the animal kingdom and that humans are the smartest creatures on the planet. So, considering the many unsolved mysteries that exist, why is the idea of there being a level of intelligence superior to our own so far-fetched or implausible for many to believe?

Where's the Logic?

I have heard it said that it takes more faith *not* to believe in God than to believe in Him. I think this is absolutely true. Doesn't it take a lot of faith in coincidence to conclude that this vast, amazing universe was formed by a "Big Bang" that produced objects out of nothing? If you know anything about the complexities of DNA, protein synthesis, and the formation of even the simplest cell, it takes a huge amount of faith to believe that one day, the right proportion of elements came together in such a perfect way to create life … and that this most basic life form eventually evolved into a human being!

On a purely intellectual level, which is the more logical explanation for creation: chance or design? To illustrate this question, I want you to imagine walking along the beach and stumbling upon an elaborate sandcastle. Would you conclude it got there by chance? Or would you assume that even though no builder was in sight, someone had carefully collected and sculpted the sand into a beautiful castle? I daresay not one person would conclude that it got there by chance ... Not one rational person would feel the need to find proof that it was built by someone because it's simply illogical to believe that the castle would just appear there by chance alone.

Unfortunately, though, believers are often harassed for believing that an unseen Designer formed the diverse and breathtaking landscapes on this earth and knit together the incredible details of the human body. I just don't understand this. To me, it's obvious that there is a Creator who is much greater and more intelligent than we are, a God who created all things intentionally for His glory.

Content With Inferiority

David expresses my thoughts about God's wisdom so well in Psalm 139:6, when he writes:

> Such knowledge is too wonderful for me, too lofty for
> me to attain.

In other words, there's simply no way for us to wrap our minds around how big God must be to create the things that we can't even fully understand. The Bible tells us that we will never be able to figure out certain mysteries because "the secret things belong to the LORD our God..." (Deuteronomy 29:29). Think about it ... If God gave away all of His secrets, He wouldn't really be God, would He?

Of course, I (along with everyone else) would love to have all the answers and be able to make sense of everything in this crazy world, and I don't think we should give up the quest to increase our knowledge and understanding about certain things. For example, I hope and pray that scientists will continue to advance their knowledge about the diseases that plague humankind and find cures and treatments to help those who suffer. However, I believe some mysteries, such as the creation of life and the universe, are better left alone. Just as it would be a waste of time for us to attempt to explain human concepts to our pets, it's simply a waste of time and effort for us to try to figure out the things of God. Since He has reserved certain things to be known only unto Him, He didn't create us with the mental capacity to figure them out. If we allow God to truly be God, I believe we can be content with the things we *do* know and trust the One who knows the rest.

I think dogs are generally good at being content—they usually seem perfectly satisfied to live their lives without trying to figure out ours. Wilbur is nosey sometimes, and occasionally he will look at an object or me inquisitively (as if he's trying to make sense of something), but typically he just minds his own business. If I'm on the computer or using the remote control to change the channels on television, Wilbur is perfectly content just lying in my lap, clueless as to what I'm doing. I have realized that I should be more like him in this respect and just leave certain unknowns in the capable hands of my Master.

Although the discrepancy of knowledge between me and Wilbur doesn't even compare to the huge discrepancy that exists between me and God, I can better understand my subordinate place and position to God through this analogy—I can better grasp the extensive difference between my intelligence and God's. Hopefully this illustration gives you greater insight into how wise God is and shows you why you should put your confidence in Him, not in man (as Psalm 118:8 advises).

We may seem like geniuses compared to our dogs, but ironically, dogs are extremely brilliant in comparison to other animals, such as frogs. There is obviously a broad and diverse range of intelligence among the creatures God has made. I believe this hierarchy of knowledge here on earth demonstrates how much greater God's level of wisdom and understanding is than our own ... He stands at the very top of the pyramid as the One and only all-knowing God.

I think it's great that unbelievers can see this concept illustrated through something as simple as relating to their pets. There is much evidence, both scientific and scriptural, that points to God and His Son, Jesus Christ. If you have doubts about God or Christianity, please take advantage of the resources that exist to help you find the Truth.[1] Remember, however, that no matter how many facts you know or how close you are to God, there will always be unanswered questions—at least until you meet the Lord face to face.

> He has also set eternity in the human heart; yet no one
> can fathom what God has done from beginning to end
> (Ecclesiastes 3:11).

---

[1] If you or someone you know is not convinced that there is a God, I strongly recommend you or they read the book, *The Case For a Creator*, by Lee Strobel, the *former* atheist and legal editor of *The Chicago Tribune*. This book is full of factual, expert advice from top scientists in various fields, from astronomy to molecular biology. It also points out the many faults with the theory of evolution. Another book by Strobel, *The Case For Christ*, is great for those who have doubts about Christianity.

Additionally, I'd recommend researching the numerous prophesies from the Old Testament, written several hundred years BC, that were fulfilled by Jesus. I also highly recommend watching the documentary, *The Star of Bethlehem*, starring Frederick A. Larson (produced by Stephen McEveety), which takes the viewer back in time, showing the positions of the stars and constellations around the time of Christ's birth and death. It's truly amazing!

CHAPTER 3: YOU FELL FOR THAT?!?

One day, as usual, I was rushing to get out the door on time, and Wilbur was relaxing on the couch, curled up in his favorite throw. I longed to leave him there and allow him full rein of the house, but that's just not an option with Wilbur; he's extremely curious, and his nose gets him into a lot of trouble! So he has to be confined to just one room of the house when he's home alone.

On this particular day, I was wearing a light-colored shirt and didn't want to pick Wilbur up and get a thousand little black hairs on it. And since I was in a hurry, I surely didn't have time to chase him around until he scooted beneath our large, square coffee table (where it's impossible to pull him out without getting on my hands and knees). So I resorted to my tried-and-true method of rounding Wilbur up. I exclaimed, "Treat!" and headed into "his room" for a few pellets of his dog food. As expected, Wilbur willingly followed me into his room with great anticipation and a wagging tail. I threw the treat on the floor, and he gobbled it down as I latched up his doggie gate.

As I completed this ritual, it occurred to me that as many times as I had done this before, Wilbur must have known that I was luring him into his room because I was preparing to leave. There's no doubt he had picked up on this simple, frequent pattern long ago. He knew I was planning to place him into mini-captivity for at least a few hours, *yet it never fails*, I thought. *He falls for it every time!*

I pondered the significance of this fact for a moment. *So,* I thought, *as Wilbur followed me to his room, he knew he was trading his freedom for a few tiny morsels of food. If I were him, I just wouldn't go for that ... not just for an itty bitty bite, for sure. That's crazy!* Then like a ton of bricks, it hit me—I had been stupid enough to do exactly the same thing many times, too. I felt the Lord whispering to my soul, *This is what it's like when you fall for the temptations of the devil.* Whoa! It's so true.

I have been lured in by the devil's schemes one too many times. There's no telling how many wonderful things I've given up by taking the bait of instant gratification ... the times I have opened my big mouth and gossiped about someone, the times I have acted out of pride or jealousy, and the list goes on and on. I'm the type of person who is extremely bothered any time something good goes to waste. So when I stopped and thought of how many blessings I've missed out on throughout my life by playing the fool, like Wilbur, it really got to me! This reality quickly opened my eyes and filled me with regret.

This should hit home with you as well, "for all have sinned and fall short of the glory of God" (Romans 3:23). Unfortunately, it's easier than ever for any one of us to slip into temptation and find ourselves in the midst of sin. It's increasingly evident that Satan is hard at work in our "anything and everything goes" society; he's chiseling away at the moral fabric which once held this nation together. I personally know many women who have enjoyed reading the bestselling book, *Fifty Shades of Grey,* by E.L. James—a book full of X-rated sexual content. So I don't have to look hard to see that evil and temptation are lurking around every corner ... on television, on the internet, in the workplace, in our families, and even in the church. Cigarettes, alcohol, drugs, materialism, pornography, and extramarital sex are all vices the devil uses to lure people away from the healthy, abundant life God wants for them. Due to the selfish and vulnerable nature of human beings, it's pretty easy for Satan to "trick" many people, including

YOU FELL FOR THAT?!?

Christians, into forfeiting many great and lasting blessings for fleeting, sinful pleasures.

The Bible states that the devil is the "father of lies" (John 8:44), but he "transforms himself into an angel of light" (2 Corinthians 11:14, NKJV). In other words, he's very sneaky. It's never been Satan's style, nor will it ever be, to show us the ugly side of sin—the real consequences of falling for his lies. No, he will always make sin look so wonderful and enticing that it's easy to ignore the voice of reason or the Voice of Truth inside us.

———

Hook, Line, and Sinker

There is a well-known story in Genesis that perfectly illustrates the consequences of giving in to instant gratification. The story is about Jacob and Esau, the twin sons of Isaac and Rebecca. Back in those days, the firstborn son received a birthright from his father. This was similar to what we think of as an inheritance. This birthright meant that the firstborn son was to assume the leadership role in the family once his father died. The birthright also entitled the firstborn son to get a double portion of the inheritance—twice what the other sons would receive. Esau, being the firstborn son (and also his father's favorite), was entitled to this privilege. He didn't seem to value this honor, however.

According to the 25th chapter of Genesis, one day Esau had been out hunting, and Jacob was at home cooking some stew. When Esau arrived home, he was tired and hungry, so he asked Jacob for a bowl of the stew he had made. Jacob, evidently seeing a good opportunity to take advantage of his brother, said he would give him some stew if Esau would swear over his birthright to him. Believe it or not, Esau actually agreed to this deal and ended up "selling" his birthright to Jacob for only a bowl of soup!

This seems preposterous to us today … How silly Esau was to give up his entire future for something so temporary. However, Esau must have been so hungry at the time that the desires of his flesh took control of him. His stomach was probably growling and crying out for a tasty, warm meal after a long day's work, and then that enticing aroma of stew greeted him at the door. At that moment of weakness, Esau obviously didn't think about the consequences of giving in to Jacob's malicious request. At the very least, he didn't take the situation seriously.

The story continues into Genesis 27, when their father, Isaac, was old and blind. It was time for Isaac to bestow his blessing, the birthright, upon Esau. Isaac was unaware of the "deal" that had taken place between his sons years before, but Rebecca and Jacob had not forgotten. Behind the scenes, Jacob and his mother, who had always favored him, devised a sneaky plan to trick Isaac. Since he was blind, they were able to disguise Jacob and deceive Isaac into believing that Jacob was Esau. And mistaking his younger son for the older one, Isaac gave Jacob the birthright.

Although he was a victim of the deceptive scheme carried out by his mother and brother, I guess Esau got what was coming to him since he did "sell" his birthright to Jacob long before for a bowl of soup. But as you can imagine, when Esau found out what had happened, he was so angry that he planned to kill his brother once his father died. Talk about family drama!

I bet that deep down, Esau was even more angry with himself for trading a moment's pleasure for a lifetime of blessings ... a mere bowl of stew for a much better, more prosperous future. The consequences were irreversible, however. There was no taking back the birthright that Isaac had already given to Jacob. While this story is a pretty extreme example of someone paying a high price for instant gratification, this type of thing happens around us all the time; it's rooted in our very nature to please ourselves in the moment and put aside thoughts of the future.

Sin = Regret

Unfortunately, the consequences we humans face from giving in to sin are usually much more serious than having to sit in a room by ourselves all day, like my dog, Wilbur. Being a nurse, I see this all the time. I see people lying on their deathbeds due to smoking-induced, end-stage emphysema or lung cancer and wonder if they regret their decision to smoke. I see people on the liver transplant waiting list due to severe alcohol-induced cirrhosis and wonder if they wish they hadn't taken to the bottle. I wonder how those who are battling AIDS due to sexual promiscuity must feel as they face death or how those who have chased material wealth feel when they are old and alone. I bet most of them have some major regrets—but then again, don't we all?

The issue of regret reminds me of the story of Judas. Think about it … Judas knew Jesus personally, in the flesh. He was one of the chosen 12 disciples, a true follower (at least in the physical sense). He and Jesus walked side by side for many a dusty mile. They were good friends who shared stories and laughs with one another, probably on a daily basis, for about three years. Judas had the privilege of watching Jesus perform miracles firsthand—the ones we only get to read about. Yet when it was all said and done, Judas's greed got the best of him, and he betrayed his Master and friend—the Son of God—for 30 pieces of silver. And almost as soon as he had completed his treacherous act, he was so guilt-ridden that he threw the pieces of silver down and hanged himself (see Matthew chapters 26-27).

Unfortunately, no amount of regret will erase the consequences of sin. We can be extremely sorry for our mistakes, confess our sins, repent, and be forgiven—thanks to God's grace and mercy through Christ. But even so, the ramifications of sin linger. They are permanently there, just like the stubborn stain on the middle of your new favorite outfit that even the dry cleaners couldn't get out.

"The Wages of Sin is Death" (Romans 6:23)

Physical death is the ultimate price of sin that plagues all of humankind. Sometimes, as in the example of Judas, sin may actually lead straight to a physical death. But there are many other kinds of death that sin causes besides the literal termination of a heartbeat. Those of you who have experienced a painful divorce know that there's an emotional death involved. When any type of meaningful relationship ends, the cold, dark, and lonely attributes of death linger near. Any time there is sexual immorality, there is a defilement of the people involved. Where bitterness, hate, and jealousy live, there is an absence—or death—of joy, love, and peace. Unfortunately, any sin, no matter how small it may seem, involves some form of death.

Sadly, even Christian people (including myself) who know these truths and understand that there will be consequences for sin give in to the devil at times. Let's be honest … sin can be fun, right? At first, sin is usually very enjoyable and satisfying to our carnal nature, and our flesh is always crying out for instant gratification. The Bible states that our human nature is in constant battle with our spirits (Galatians 5:17). This means that there truly is a war going on inside of believers essentially all the time. When thinking about this, I can't help but picture the cartoon or comic book characters who have the devil floating on one side of their heads and an angel on the other. I guess this is a pretty accurate depiction of what's going on inside of us at any given moment.

Every day we must make many decisions that basically come down to one choice: Do we take the challenging high road that we know is right, or do we compromise our beliefs and take the easier way out? Unfortunately, these decisions are usually very hard to make. As the Bible says, "the spirit is willing, but the flesh is weak" (Matthew 26:41). And the devil is an experienced, ruthless tempter. Scripture warns us:

> Be alert and of sober mind. Your enemy the devil prowls around like a roaring lion looking for someone to devour (1 Peter 5:8).

If you stop and really contemplate this, it's very unnerving. At least I find it to be. The thought of the most evil force in existence lurking around every corner, anxiously waiting for me to slip up so that he can rip me apart, is like a real-life horror movie! Even though physical bloodshed or harm is not frequently involved, the work of the devil is serious business.

○══════╸

Victory on the Battlefield

Entire books have been written on spiritual warfare, but the following passage from Ephesians sums up the basic principles of fighting the battle against sin:

> Finally, be strong in the Lord and in his mighty power. Put on the full armor of God, so that you can take your stand against the devil's schemes. For our struggle is not against flesh and blood, but against the rulers, against the authorities, against the powers of this dark world and against the spiritual forces of evil in the heavenly realms. Therefore, put on the full armor of God, so that when the day of evil comes, you may be able to stand your ground, and after you have done everything, to stand. Stand firm then, with the belt of truth buckled around your waist, with the breastplate of righteousness in place, and with your feet fitted with the readiness that comes from the gospel of peace. In addition to all this, take up the shield of faith, with which you can extinguish all the flaming arrows of the evil one. Take the helmet of salvation and the sword of the Spirit, which is the word of God. And pray in the Spirit on all occasions with all kinds of prayers

and requests. With this in mind, be alert and always keep on praying for all the Lord's people (Ephesians 6:10-18).

When I think of how often we carelessly "toy" with sin, I can't help but think of the song "Danger Zone" from the popular movie *Top Gun*. The old saying "when you play with fire, you're going to get burned" also comes to mind. I believe we need to take God's warnings about sin more seriously and that we should take an aggressive stance against it. Fortunately, Christ has provided us with an arsenal of effective weapons to use for our battle against sin. It's important that we're familiar with these spiritual weapons and that we feel comfortable, even confident, using them. If not, we'll end up playing the fool, just like my Wilbur, and forfeit many eternal blessings for Satan's temporary treats.

The following are some powerful verses of Scripture that go along with the topics in this chapter. You can refer to them to help you be on guard and fight the good fight. Perhaps write them down, along with the other verses included in this chapter, and carry them around with you. Better yet, memorize them. From my experience, I can tell you that if you have immediate access to applicable Scriptures in your mind and heart, you'll be even better prepared for battle.

> This day I call the heavens and the earth as witnesses against you that I have set before you life and death, blessings and curses. Now choose life, so that you and your children may live (Deuteronomy 30:19).

> But each one is tempted when he is drawn away by his own desires and enticed. Then, when desire has conceived, it gives birth to sin; and sin, when it is full-grown, brings forth death. Do not be deceived, my beloved brethren (James 1:14-16, NKJV).

Submit yourselves, then, to God. Resist the devil, and he will flee from you (James 4:7).

And let us not grow weary while doing good, for in due season we shall reap if we do not lose heart (Galatians 6:9, NKJV).

No temptation has overtaken you except what is common to mankind. And God is faithful; he will not let you be tempted beyond what you can bear. But when you are tempted, he will also provide a way out so that you can endure it (1 Corinthians 10:13).

I am so thankful God revealed to me the analogy regarding my "Wilbur mentality." As a result, I am now more cautious in regards to my vulnerabilities and weaknesses. I'm also better equipped to anticipate when, where, and how my enemy will strike, and I feel more empowered to defend myself against him. I guess it's a bit prideful, but I can't stand the thought of the devil robbing me of a blessing and exclaiming, "*Ha, ha, ha, you sucker ... you fell for that again!*" I hope this analogy benefits you as well. I want you to be on guard against your enemy and realize the serious repercussions that can come from *each and every* sin.

In conclusion, please pray this prayer:

Dear God,

Please help me identify my weaknesses and the evil that exists in my life. Help me stay spiritually strong in Christ and alert my spirit to the devil's schemes to destroy me. Please give me the will to rebuke him and the strength to choose life instead of death and blessings instead of curses. I want to resist falling "hook, line, and sinker" for the bait Satan throws my way so that, instead of shortchanging myself for fleeting pleasures that drag me down the road of regret and despair, I can enjoy Your wonderful, everlasting blessings.

In the holy and powerful name of Your Son, Jesus Christ,

Amen.

CHAPTER 4: I KNOW WHO YOU ARE!

If you're a dog owner, you know that dogs can do some pretty crazy things. Think about it: Are you really surprised to see your dog running through the house with a dirty pair of underwear, acting as if he's just found buried treasure? What about when you find your dog scavenging through the garbage, chasing his tail, or sniffing every square inch of another dog? You may be disgusted by some of these typical doggie behaviors or habits, but I seriously doubt you're surprised by any of them. Wilbur has certainly pulled his share of gross and mischievous stunts, and I overlook most of them because I realize that dogs will be dogs. Consider this memorable example of one of Wilbur's exploits ...

One day I was home doing housework, and Wilbur was just hanging out in our living room as usual. I went into the laundry room for all of about five minutes to get some clothes out of the dryer. When I came back into the living room, I noticed that a large pack of chewing gum was missing from the center of the coffee table. I began to question how Wilbur could've jumped high or far enough to reach the gum and wondered whether the pack of gum had really been there at all.

As I looked around the house, I didn't see any evidence of gum anywhere ... no aluminum wrappers or cardboard packaging, and definitely no gum. Still, I was 99.9 percent sure that the gum had been there. So my heart started racing—I knew I had chewed only two or three pieces, so if Wilbur had gotten the gum, that meant there were at least 12 pieces, along with aluminum wrappers and exterior packaging, that he could have eaten! I knew I needed to act quickly in case something in the gum or wrappers could be toxic to him.

I frantically called the vet, and sure enough, they said I needed to bring Wilbur in to have his stomach pumped! It turns out that there is a substance called xylitol in many sugar-free chewing gums that can cause major liver damage. So I rushed Wilbur to the vet, where they gave him medication to induce vomiting. We waited and waited, and I grew more worried as the minutes passed. Just as the veterinarian said he might have to resort to something else to get him to vomit, poor Wilbur started retching. I could see his stomach muscles contracting as he threw up time after time. My suspicion was confirmed; there on the floor lay piles and piles of pink, watermelon-smelling vomit intermingled with shiny pieces of aluminum! (The vet assistant said it was the best-smelling vomit she had ever smelled!) And there was poor Wilbur, sprawled out on the floor, breathing heavily. It was obvious that he was completely spent and feeling pretty rough. He definitely found out that the gum was much more fun going down than coming back up! He paid a high price for those few moments of pleasure, as did I when I paid the vet's bill.

Unfortunately, this wasn't the last time Wilbur would find himself in a similar situation, despite our best efforts to prevent them. Once, my husband's travel bag must have fallen out of the closet unnoticed while I was hanging up some clothes, and Wilbur helped himself to a plastic baggie full of Tums and Tylenol! He's also chewed *through* my purse before to eat chocolate and gum. (He obviously *loves* chewing gum, especially watermelon-flavored!) My husband and I have now learned how to handle these types of emergencies ourselves with a little hydrogen peroxide, but each time, it's a horrible ordeal. I don't think I've ever felt guiltier than when

I have had to force that nasty, foaming hydrogen peroxide down Wilbur's throat!

The reason I've told you about Wilbur getting into trouble is to better illustrate the next analogy I want to share. You see, I've never been angry with Wilbur for any of the drama he has caused—not even considering the money we've forked out as a result. Sure, I was plenty frustrated and upset. But there's no way I can blame Wilbur for just being a dog. I couldn't expect him to turn down an opportunity to scarf down something tasty behind my back because it's just part of his nature to snoop around and try to find something good to eat.

After Wilbur's gum incident, it occurred to me that there could be a distinct parallel between the way I feel toward Wilbur when he gets into trouble and the way God feels toward me when I sin. No more than a second after I began to contemplate this, a Scripture flashed through my mind:

> As a father pities his children, so the Lord pities those who fear Him. For He knows our frame; He remembers that we are dust (Psalm 103:13-14, NKJV).

This Scripture was my confirmation that God looks at me and my sinful nature much like I look at Wilbur after he pulls a mischievous stunt. Since God created me, He's fully aware that I'm a sinful, trouble-bound creature; He realizes that sin is inescapable for me because it's rooted in my very nature ... That's why He carried out the plan of redemption through His only righteous Son.

Knowing that God expects me to mess up occasionally and that He has compassion upon me in my states of weakness has given me a freeing sense of peace. Isn't it amazing that none of our wild diversions from God's path have caught Him by surprise? God knows why each of us has the problems, weaknesses, and temptations we have. He realizes that it's simply natural for us to experience emotions such as anger, jealousy, insecurity, lust, and pride—just as natural as the earth we're formed of. It's so nice to know that God knows us through and through—that He truly *gets* us.

———

Caught Red-Handed

Picture this scenario: A six-year-old child has been forbidden by his parents to use knives. He, of course, doesn't like being told what he can and can't do. He longs to prove his independence, so he defies the rule. While cutting an apple, he injures himself, nearly severing the tip of his finger. He begins to scream and cry, and he runs to his mother for help. How do you think his mother will react? Will she respond with anger toward her son for disobeying her rules? Or will she address his wound and try to soothe his tears?

We all know that the typical mother in this situation will come to her son's rescue, having compassion on him in this moment of extreme pain. She will try to stop the bleeding and do her best to comfort her son as she rushes him to the emergency room, silently worrying and praying the whole way there. In times like these, sympathy, compassion, and concern prevail over anger and frustration (initially, at least). So why would a loving God feel any differently toward His children in the midst of their troubles, even when those troubles are caused by their disobedience?

It's common knowledge that children will rebel against their parents and the rules from time to time. It's simply normal for children to push limits and test boundaries. And when something bad happens as a result of a child's disobedience, parents continue to love that child in the midst of their disappointment. Similarly, I believe that even when we deliberately choose to disobey God, His love for us remains steady.

Even though I am just the "parent" of a dachshund, I feel like I can see both God's frustration with disobedience and His compassion for sinners much more clearly when I look at things through the eyes of a parent. For both parents and pet owners, rules and discipline are enforced out of love and protection. I believe it's the same with God ... He has given us certain rules to abide by because He loves us and wants to keep us from getting hurt—not because He just wants to shake His finger in our faces or to flaunt His superiority.

I imagine that God grieves when we sin because we have inflicted harm upon ourselves, and it saddens Him to watch us suffer. He wants us to stay on the right path where we are under His umbrella of supernatural protection and provision. It makes total sense for God to discipline us and allow us to deal with the consequences of sin in order to prevent us from inflicting further harm upon ourselves. God's discipline is surely an act of love, as His Word says:

> Those whom I love I rebuke and discipline (Revelation 3:19).

Get Real!

Let's face it: God knows everything we do and everything we say. Perhaps most frightening is that He knows everything we think, too. Since we can't hide from God, I believe the only logical thing we can do is to be completely real with Him.

I don't know of many things that bug me more than listening to people use elevated speech (what I call their "holier than thou" voice) to pray. I absolutely cringe when those high and mighty words begin to flow! If you've spent much time in church, you probably recognize that tone ... You might have even used it yourself when called upon to pray. This behavior toward prayer frustrates me because when people do this, I feel like they're trying to "pull the wool over" God's eyes, which, of course, is impossible! A person may be able to fool other people, but he will never sneak anything past an all-knowing God.

My suspicion is that some people assume this kind of prayerful affectation, not with the intention of faking anything, but because they feel disconnected from God—or perhaps they feel unworthy to talk to Him in a conversational tone. Whatever the reason, it makes no sense for anybody to be anything other than their true selves with God because He knows us even better than we know our own selves. We should always be reverent toward God and have an appropriate fear of Him, yet we must be authentic when we come to Him as well. Unlike other faiths, Christianity is centered around God's love, grace, and mercy; and being truthful is the first step in obtaining God's grace and mercy. You must be willing to acknowledge and confess your sins, and *then* "the truth will set you free" (John 8:32).

One night, after struggling with some thoughts and feelings centered around insecurity and envy, I just decided to let it all out. I started crying as I washed my face and began speaking the truths of my heart aloud to God. I poured out my feelings to Him as if He were sitting right in front of me. I looked in the mirror and cried out, "God, only **You** know—no one else really understands! You're the *only* One who has been with me every second of my life; You're the *only* One that truly gets me and knows why I feel the way I do; and You're the *only* One who can help me deal with this."

I can't express just how freeing it was to actually hear myself saying these things to God. I no longer felt alone with my sinful, conflicting thoughts and feelings. I knew God could read my mind and heart, but speaking to Him as if I were speaking to another human made Him seem so much closer and more "real." Standing in front of the mirror and watching myself speak to God made it even better, perhaps because so many of my physical senses were engaged in this experience. All I know is that I felt a great sense of release and relief afterwards, and I viewed God as my best friend like never before.

I find it sad that many people don't realize that God can be both their Lord *and* their friend. I think many people relate to God as if He were a strict drill sergeant; they seem to walk on eggshells before Him or shy away from a genuine relationship with Him because they think He expects perfect behavior. Naturally, they feel guilty about their sins, but instead of running toward God, they withdraw, thinking He is fuming with anger and ready to strike them down at any second. If you are one of those who view God in any of these ways, I hope and pray that you'll begin to develop a different image of Him.

While we all have negative thoughts and feelings that we hide from others, we should embrace the fact that there is Someone who completely understands us. Instead of being embarrassed or feeling unworthy of God's love because of our secret faults and sins, we should be heartened that He knows these unspeakable things and yet loves us just the same! Our Creator knows that in our flesh we are nothing more than glorified dirt, incapable of living moral lives; He realizes that it's only by and through His Holy Spirit inside of us that we are able to truly do good. In other words, God *gets* that we—just like Wilbur—have a tendency to "snoop around" and get into trouble.

When you mess up (despite your best efforts, it's just a matter of time), I hope you will do as I do and recall the analogy of Wilbur and the chewing gum and be reassured of God's continued love for you. When you are "sprawled out on the floor," suffering the consequences of sin, know that God has compassion upon you and that He disciplines you out of love. He just wants you to be real with Him by acknowledging your sinfulness and your need for His redeeming grace.

I'm going to conclude this chapter with Psalm 103 in its entirety. It's one of my favorite Psalms and gave me the inspiration for this chapter:

> Praise the LORD, my soul;
> all my inmost being, praise his holy name.
> Praise the LORD, my soul,
> and forget not all his benefits—
> who forgives all your sins
> and heals all your diseases,
> who redeems your life from the pit

and crowns you with love and compassion,
who satisfies your desires with good things
so that your youth is renewed like the eagle's.

The LORD works righteousness
and justice for all the oppressed.

He made known his ways to Moses,
his deeds to the people of Israel:
The LORD is compassionate and gracious,
slow to anger, abounding in love.
He will not always accuse,
nor will he harbor his anger forever;
he does not treat us as our sins deserve
or repay us according to our iniquities.
For as high as the heavens are above the earth,
so great is his love for those who fear him;
as far as the east is from the west,
so far has he removed our transgressions from us.

As a father has compassion on his children,
so the LORD has compassion on those who fear him;
for he knows how we are formed,
he remembers that we are dust.
The life of mortals is like grass,
they flourish like a flower of the field;
the wind blows over it and it is gone,
and its place remembers it no more.
But from everlasting to everlasting
the LORD's love is with those who fear him,
and his righteousness with their children's children—
with those who keep his covenant
and remember to obey his precepts.

The LORD has established his throne in heaven,
and his kingdom rules over all.

Praise the LORD, you his angels,
you mighty ones who do his bidding,
who obey his word.
Praise the LORD, all his heavenly hosts,
you his servants who do his will.
Praise the LORD, all his works
everywhere in his dominion.

Praise the LORD, my soul (Psalm 103).

CHAPTER 5: CHOICE LOVE

Have you ever felt like a burden to someone? I imagine we all have at one time or another. As I write this, I'm recuperating from a stomach virus, so I've felt like a burden for several days. I missed work and felt terrible knowing that my coworkers would struggle to find another nurse to cover for me, and my husband has had to wait on me hand and foot. Although I had no other choice than to call out of work and be dependent upon care, I can't stand feeling like such an inconvenience to others.

One time when Wilbur was sick, I think he felt like a burden, too. He had thrown up several times and watched as I cleaned up after him. I looked over at him and saw a very sad, humble look in his eyes. He looked so submissive, his head lowered and his tail tucked beneath his legs. I had the impression that he was, in his own way, apologizing to me. Though I'm not certain that animals are capable of feeling guilt or "apologizing," I sure did feel compassion for Wilbur in that moment.

So I put down the paper towels, took him in my arms, and snuggled him, praying he would be back to his normal self again soon. I wanted to reassure Wilbur that I loved him and that he wasn't a burden to me. I also wanted him to know that I chose to love him and take care of him … and that's the reason we got him in the first place. Sure, we wanted a dog for the love and companionship that he could give to us, but we wanted to shower him with love as well. I'm sure many of you feel the same way about your pets or children.

Sometimes Wilbur does some funny things to get his needs met. For example, if we overlook that his water bowl is empty, he takes that long snout of his and pushes his bowl so that it makes a loud clanking noise. I'll never forget a day several years ago when I was sick with the flu, lying almost lifeless on the couch as I watched episode after episode of *Little House on the Prairie*. Wilbur, being the loyal friend he is, stayed right beside me for hours. Eventually, though, he got down from the couch and went in the next room to get a drink of water. I then heard the bowl clanking, and I thought, *Oh, great ... I guess I have to get up now!*

I wanted to get up and be attentive—I really did. But I felt *so* bad and just couldn't muster up enough energy to drag myself off the couch. I know it sounds terrible, but I thought I could let it slide for a while. I knew Wilbur wasn't going to die of dehydration if he didn't get a drink of water right that second, so I continued to lie there, hoping he would just forget about it. Boy was I wrong!

Being the dachshund he is, Wilbur is extremely persistent. He clanked his bowl a few more times without success, and the next thing I knew, Wilbur was standing right in front of me with the mat that holds his bowls between his teeth! He had pulled the mat (along with his ceramic food and water bowls) about 15 feet to show me what he wanted. I couldn't believe Wilbur was that smart and determined, and I felt so bad that he had to go to such drastic measures to get a drink of water; he was obviously very thirsty! Of course, at that point I couldn't hesitate a moment longer, so I dragged myself off the couch to get my baby some water!

Loving to Love

Obviously, Wilbur is well-aware that my husband and I are his lifelines. He is completely dependent upon our care, and I don't mind that at all. In fact, I thoroughly enjoy being Wilbur's provider and caretaker. Loving Wilbur, like loving anyone, is sometimes inconvenient (I don't enjoy cleaning up his messes!), but those times don't diminish the joy I get from our relationship—not even a little bit. I actually find it very rewarding that Wilbur needs me for essentially everything; I like being depended upon. It makes me feel valuable to know that I can meet the needs of such a precious creature and make his life worthwhile.

I thoroughly enjoy watching Wilbur's expression light up and his tail wag super-fast when I exclaim, "Dinner!" I also love to give Wilbur new toys and watch his eyes widen with excitement and his ears perk up with curiosity. I'm sure you fellow animal-lovers can relate, and those of you who are parents must experience an even greater amount of satisfaction and joy from providing for your children.

I think nearly everyone finds fulfillment in caring for and bringing joy to others, especially their loved ones. Even little girls enjoy "caring for" their dolls, and young boys love to imitate heroic figures who help others. I believe this desire, this need to nurture, is planted within us by God. We are made in God's image, and the Bible says that He loves and longs to care for His children ... He actually wants to gather and protect His children "as a hen gathers her chicks under her wings" (Mathew 23:37). This verse certainly suggests that it pleases God to care for and protect His children. I believe it also implies that He and many of the creatures He created experience similar feelings of satisfaction and fulfillment when caring for others.

So, how does it feel to think of God longing to protect and nurture you? It humbles me to think that the Creator of the universe takes pleasure in caring for me—every second of every minute of every hour of every day of my life. It moves me to think that His care and provision over me isn't a matter of Him feeling obligated to do these things ... It's actually His true desire, just as it's my desire to tend to Wilbur.

It makes sense that we feel burdensome to others from time to time when we require much attention and care from them. We know that people are only capable of handling so much, being limited in patience, energy, and resources. It's very different with God, however, because He's not limited in any way. Psalm 121:3-4 tells us:

> He will not let your foot slip—he who watches over you will not slumber; indeed, he who watches over Israel will neither slumber nor sleep.

Isn't it wonderful to think that we never need to feel like a burden to God ... that we can depend on Him *wanting* to help us at any time, day or night? I find it very reassuring to know that I can never exhaust God—that He has an endless supply of love, energy, and attentiveness. I hope you can find comfort, as I do, in knowing that there is Someone who never needs or wants a break from you—not even to sleep and not even when you sleep. It's quite likely that God, like a doting parent rocking a sleeping baby (or me holding Wilbur as he sleeps in my arms), finds much delight in simply watching you in peaceful slumber. Think about that. It's amazing that the Creator of the universe adores us this much!

***

Love = Blessings + Sacrifice

We all know that love inspires and motivates us to give ... of ourselves, our time, and our resources. In my opinion, there aren't many greater feelings in the world than the feeling of giving someone I love a gift they genuinely enjoy. Just as I love giving that "perfect" gift to someone (including Wilbur), I believe God finds much pleasure in lavishing gifts upon His children. In fact, the Bible tells us that God is the expert gift-giver. Matthew 7:11 states:

> If you, then, though you are evil, know how to give
> good gifts to your children, how much more will your
> Father in heaven give good gifts to those who ask him!

The giving of gifts is simply an outpouring of love, and God is definitely the expert on love. He loves us so much that He gave up His one and only Son, and Jesus endured immeasurable emotional and physical pain as He sacrificed His very life in order to save us. This is truly the best gift of love that has ever been given. Jesus was completely selfless in His sacrifice.[2]

Considering God's demonstration of love, it's evident that true love involves sacrifice. If we're honest, most of us can't stand the word *sacrifice*, much less the principle, right? Giving up anything on behalf of another is contrary to our selfish, fleshly nature. But when you deeply love someone, it's not so hard to put aside your own wants and needs to care for them. For instance, most parents expect to put their children ahead of themselves the majority of the time. Yet Jesus makes it clear that His commandment to love our neighbors as ourselves doesn't just mean that we're to love our family and friends as ourselves. He asks:

> If you love those who love you, what credit is that to
> you? Even sinners love those who love them. And if
> you do good to those who are good to you, what credit
> is that to you? Even sinners do that. And if you lend to
> those from whom you expect repayment, what credit
> is that to you? Even sinners lend to sinners, expecting
> to be repaid in full (Luke 6:32-34).

---

[2] If you've never seen the movie *Passion of the Christ*, I highly recommend you see it to get an *idea* of the sacrifice Jesus made out of love for you.

Obviously, the true test of Christian love is doing good to people we don't have relationships with and giving to people who will never repay us. Jesus demonstrated true love by dying for people who will never love Him in return—people who actually hate and mock Him.

Out of gratitude to God for the sacrifice He made for us, I believe the least we should do to "pay it forward" is to give up some of our time and money to help others. I don't know about you, but I could stand to improve in this area. I tithe and donate money to good causes, but I know I should and could do more. There are billions of people in the world who can't even take a sip of water without worrying about contracting a deadly illness, yet I often go shopping and buy myself a new purse or a new pair of shoes to add to my abundant collection. We who are blessed could change, even save, lives by sacrificing more of the trivial things we *want* in order to meet others' *needs*.

I realize that I've gone off on a bit of a tangent here, but I feel like we often need reminding of what true love really is in order to fully appreciate God's love for us. Christians are privileged to enjoy the many wonderful gifts and blessings that God wants to give us. May we never forget that true love involves both blessings *and* sacrifice.

Feel the Love

It comes as no surprise to most Christians that God is loving and giving, so I hope I haven't tired you with so much talk about God's love. However, I believe this is a fundamental concept that you must grasp in order to grow spiritually and nurture a deeper relationship with Christ.

Even though I was raised with the teachings of God's love and had John 3:16 memorized for years, I didn't really *get it* until I thought of God's love for me in light of Wilbur. I'm not saying that God loves me (or us) in the exact same way that I love my dog! However, I better understand the depth of God's love in light of my unconditional love for

Wilbur. It feels so good to picture God deliberately picking me out to be His child (just as I excitedly picked out Wilbur to be my little companion) and to know that He enjoys providing for me, even when I'm a burden to someone else.

In the past, I pictured God providing for my needs and occasionally granting my requests without having much emotion involved ... much like a sales associate at a department store would help me locate something and ring me up at the register. But since I received this insight from my Wilbur analogy, I've been able to see God's love for me on a much more personal level, and this revelation has really enhanced my relationship with Him. I have a feeling many of you are in need of a new, more accurate perspective of God's love for you as well.

I want to share with you a verse in the Bible that perfectly illustrates the point I want you to take away from this message:

> For the LORD your God is living among you. He is a mighty savior. He will take delight in you with gladness. With his love, he will calm all your fears. He will rejoice over you with joyful songs (Zephaniah 3:17, NLT).

Please reread this verse and allow the words to soak into your heart. If you are His child, the God of the universe takes delight in you—so much so that He even sings for joy! Isn't that amazing? You may feel like a nobody. Perhaps someone has even told you that you're not worthy of being loved. However, if God—the most powerful, loving Force in all existence—delights in you, you better believe you are important and loved!

Imagine God running to meet you any time you approach Him, with open arms and excitement, like the father in the parable of the prodigal son (found in Luke 15). Think of God longing to take you under His wings of love and protection, much like you yearn to shelter and pamper your children or pets. Be encouraged and blessed to know that you—yes, YOU—are that special to Him. Just because God loves multitudes of people doesn't mean that He can't single you out and love and bless you in a totally individualized way.

Basically, the point I want to get across to you is this: God *loves* loving you! He definitely doesn't love you out of duty since He is subject to no rules and is bound to no obligations. He *wants* and *chooses* to love you. He *desires* to protect you, to provide for you, and to shower you with gifts—even more than we want to do these things for the people and pets we love. Be convinced … **God *loves* loving you!**

In conclusion, I pray this prayer over you:

> *Dear God,*
>
> *I pray that each reader of this book and all of Your children may truly understand how special they are. I ask that if they ever feel unlovable or like a burden, that they will remember and reflect upon these concepts and analogies about Your awesome love. I ask that You refresh their souls with the assurance that You purposefully and gladly chose them, and that You love them and take more pleasure in them than they can ever imagine. I also ask that they pass Your love on to others.*

My prayer continues with the same prayer that Paul prayed for the Ephesians:

> I pray that out of his glorious riches he may strengthen you with power through his Spirit in your inner being, so that Christ may dwell in your hearts through faith. And I pray that you, being *rooted and established in love*, may have power, together with all the Lord's holy people, to grasp *how wide and long and high and deep is the love*

of Christ, and to know this love that surpasses knowledge—
that you may be filled to the measure of all the fullness
of God (Ephesians 3:16-19, emphasis mine).

In the Mighty name of Jesus, I pray,

Amen.

CHAPTER 6: UNDERSTANDING PRAYER

Unanswered Prayers

If anyone has reason to believe her dog will go to Heaven, I do. Do you know why? That's because my Wilbur is a "praying" dog! (Look again at the cover of this book if you don't believe me!) He stands up on his hind legs and holds his two front paws together in a stance of prayer. From an early age, Wilbur started begging for food by standing on his hind legs. He got this down pat, as many dogs do, and he would sit on his haunches for a few minutes straight. One day, I guess he thought we weren't taking him seriously enough, so Wilbur added some motion to his begging by bringing his front paws together. I thought it was so precious and wanted him to continue doing this, so I rewarded this behavior consistently and said "Pray!" each time he did it. So even though he doesn't need this instruction, he now "prays" on command.

Each and every time Wilbur "prays," he looks so adorable, and it absolutely melts my heart! Even still, sometimes his "prayers" must go unanswered. You see, my husband and I generally don't give Wilbur table scraps. We would love to, but the vet advised us not to do this—and for good reason. We found out the hard way that Wilbur has an ultra-sensitive stomach. We once spent a small fortune on treating gastritis caused by him eating a potato chip or two that fell on the floor;

therefore, we're strict with what we allow Wilbur to eat. At meal-
times, we usually keep a stash of crackers or carrots nearby and give
him tiny pieces each time he "prays." Or sometimes we break off small
pieces of bread for him from something we are eating. In other words,
we typically give Wilbur *something* when he "prays."

It breaks my heart when I'm eating something like chocolate (which
he definitely shouldn't have) and I don't have anything to give him when
he begs. He looks up at me with the saddest, questioning expression in
his eyes, "praying" to no avail. It's pitiful! I know Wilbur doesn't understand why I can't give him a bite of what I'm eating, and I feel terrible
thinking that he probably believes I'm ignoring him or that I just don't
care about his "request."

One time when this situation occurred, I saw a correlation
between my relationship with Wilbur and my relationship with God.
I felt the Holy Spirit saying, *This feeling that you have toward Wilbur when
he wants something from you that you can't give him is similar to the way I feel
when I can't give you something you're asking Me for. You see, it's not that I
don't care about you and your requests, and I'm certainly not ignoring you ...
Actually, it's just the opposite, and it breaks My heart for you to think otherwise. It's simply that I love you too much to give you what you want sometimes
because I know that it will be harmful to you or that it's just not right for you
or My purposes.*

It was so comforting to feel God speaking this truth to my soul,
even though it wasn't a huge revelation for me because I had been taught
this concept about unanswered prayers for practically my entire life.
Actually, one of my favorite songs is "Unanswered Prayers," made
famous by country artist Garth Brooks. I have often found comfort in
the words of this song, which tells the story of a man who is thankful that God blessed him by *not* answering his prayers in the past. The
man in the song now has a treasured relationship with a wonderful
wife, which he would've missed if God had allowed him to be with the
woman he originally wanted in high school. I think we all like to be
reminded that if God doesn't give us what we ask for, it's because He

has something even better planned for us down the road. It also helps to believe the popular saying about God opening a door when He shuts a window.

Yet, even if we believe in God's provision, the pain and questions that come from unanswered prayers can seem overwhelming at times. As a hospice nurse, I'm confronted with tragic, difficult-to-understand situations much too often. I see the harsh realities that people deal with as a result of God not answering prayer the way we think He should. It's hard, even as Christians, not to question God sometimes—especially when we want something so badly and don't see how the granting of our request could be anything but good. I mean, why doesn't God heal a young Christian mother who is dying of cancer? There could be nothing but good to come from her healing, we rationalize. Naturally, we question God when He chooses to take this woman home at the age of 31, leaving her young child, devoted husband, and many loved ones to suffer such great loss. As I emphasized in previous chapters, our knowledge and understanding are so limited compared to God's, and this analogy of unanswered prayer stems off of that point.

Fortunately, God gives us many blessings in place of our denied requests. I think we can all relate to the message of "Unanswered Prayers," being glad that God didn't give us everything we wanted in the past. I know I'm thankful to God for not answering some of my prayers. What about you? Can you think of some examples in your life where God ended up blessing you by *not* giving you something you asked Him for? If so, I think it's important that you remember and reflect upon these things from time to time. During trying times when we aren't receiving what we ask from God, it's beneficial to recall what God has done for us in the past ... that way, we can be reassured that He will pull us through again. I believe this can be an instant faith lift!

Intentions

In the book of James, the author gives us a direct reason why God doesn't always give us what we ask Him for. James writes:

> When you ask, you do not receive, because you ask with wrong motives, that you may spend what you get on your pleasures (James 4:3).

Ouch! How true that often is. Many times, we request things from God out of pure selfishness, right? The Bible clearly states this is why we don't receive some of the things we ask God for. If you haven't gotten your desired answer to prayer, perhaps you need to evaluate your motives for asking God for it in the first place. We must face the fact that our motives are never hidden from God; He sees straight into our hearts. God wants us to continually grow more mature in Christ ... He wants our hearts to look more like His. Consequently, God has reason to deny any request that we ask of Him which involves mere selfishness.

Jesus tells us these things concerning prayer:

> This is the confidence we have in approaching God: that if we ask anything according to his will, he hears us (1 John 5:14).

> But if you remain in me and my words remain in you, you may ask for anything you want, and it will be granted! (John 15:7, NLT).

If we want answers to our prayers, it's obviously very important for us to remain close to God and pray according to His will. Did you notice the "ifs" in the verses above? Perhaps IF we always stay close to God and His Word, our desires will change and become less self-centered; perhaps our desires and prayers will line up with His will.

I believe the moral of the story is this: the more our hearts begin to look like God's heart, the more prayers we'll see answered in our lives.

Persistence Pays Off

In one sense, prayer is rather simple. At its heart, prayer is just communicating your thoughts, feelings, and/or requests to God. However, I think some aspects of prayer are complex. For instance, sometimes it may appear that God has said "No" to a particular request when, actually, He has said "Wait."

Jesus told his disciples a parable about a widow who persistently came before an unjust judge, pleading for justice against her adversary. For no legitimate reason, the judge repeatedly denied the widow justice. But she didn't give up and continued bringing her case before the judge. Finally, the judge got so bothered by the widow's persistent pleading that he gave her what she asked for. Jesus told the disciples this parable "to show them that they should always pray and not give up" (Luke 18:1); for if an *unjust* judge could be persuaded to bring forth justice, they could be certain that a *just* God will attend to the persevering pleas of His people.

In Matthew 7:7, the Bible again states the need for tenacity in our prayer lives:

> *Keep on* asking, and you will receive what you ask for. *Keep on* seeking, and you will find. *Keep on* knocking, and the door will be opened to you (NLT, emphasis mine).

Obviously, God values persistence. We admire people like the widow in the above story—people who refuse to give up on their hopes and dreams. So it makes sense that God esteems this characteristic as well.

I believe God finally brought me and my ex-husband together due to my persistent prayers for this to transpire. It's embarrassing to admit this, but I prayed for him to fall in love with me for several years. Even though God knew that the final outcome of our relationship wouldn't be what I had hoped, He had His reasons for finally answering my prayers and bringing us together.

Sometimes I wonder if God gives us what we persistently ask Him for, even when it isn't His perfect will for us, because He knows we are too stubborn to move forward otherwise. I suspect that God had to allow me to figure out for myself what He already knew in order for me to let go of my agenda and move on toward the blessings He had in store for me. I also believe God granted my request because He knew that I would learn and grow from the experience; He knew it would eventually bring me closer to Him and help mold me into the woman He wants me to be. These rationales make sense to me, but only God knows the real reason (or reasons) He eventually answered my persistent prayers.

I think there are also times when God desires and intends to give us *exactly* what we ask Him for, but only in His timing and not a moment sooner. Perhaps He wants to test our faith or make us wait so that we will appreciate Him and His blessings more when He finally answers our prayers. Whatever His reasons, I believe a significant lesson for us is this: If God is clearly not opening the doors we have repeatedly prayed for Him to open—even when the motives of our hearts are pure—we should accept that it may not be within His will to grant our requests. However, we should *keep on* hoping that He will answer our prayers and be persistent in our asking.

Be Bold

Another important concept when it comes to prayer is found in Hebrews 4:16. The New International Version translates the verse like this:

Let us then approach God's throne of grace with confidence, so that we may receive mercy and find grace to help us in our time of need.

The New Living Translation puts it this way:

So let us come boldly to the throne of our gracious God. There we will receive his mercy, and we will find grace to help us when we need it most.

Confidence and boldness. It's clear from this verse in Hebrews that God values these qualities when it comes to our expectations of Him. He hung the moon and placed every star in the sky, calling them by name (Isaiah 40:26), so I believe it's understandable why He wants His children to have complete confidence in His ability to answer prayer. He doesn't want us approaching Him sheepishly, like a timid dog with its tail tucked between its legs. No! Instead, He wants us to have so much faith in Him that we come **boldly** with our requests, fully confident in His ability to do anything.

I find it very funny that Wilbur, typically being so sweet and humble, will quickly change his tune when he *really* wants something. This may sound crazy, but at times he will give me "the look"—an unmistakably bold, expectant stare. He gets in his "prayer stance," looks deep into my eyes, and perks his ears in a way that almost makes him look threatening! He exudes a strong sense of entitlement in his expression, as if he's thinking and saying, *You BETTER give me some of that!*

You may think this is silly and far-fetched, but he really comes across that way sometimes. The funny thing is that this approach actually works for him because when he gives me that particular look, I feel like he's holding me accountable to something; I feel that I'm obligated to fulfill his expectations of me. He's pretty smooth!

There are also times when I don't give Wilbur a bite of something I'm eating and he charges me, getting right up in my face or my food, refusing to take "No" for an answer! I can't believe how assertive and demanding he can be when he really wants something! I guess he has the right idea because the bold approach always works for him. It works for us, too, according to Hebrews 4:16, which is why we should be more confident as we bring our requests before God. I don't mean that we should be threatening to God—far from it! However, we should bring our requests to Him confidently and assertively, being fully expectant of blessings from our Heavenly Father.

Prayer is a topic of great importance in the life of every believer. In fact, it's a fundamental concept of the Christian faith. I believe that our success with prayer depends largely upon how well we maintain our faith and hope in God in the midst of uncertainty. Hebrews 11:1 says that "faith is the substance of things *hoped for*, the evidence of things not seen" (NKJV, emphasis mine). Prayer provides us the opportunity to cling to hope—the hope, or expectation, that God will work things out for our good. Even when our prayers aren't answered, we still need not be hopeless; we must simply shift our hope in another direction. When we put our hope and faith in God's plans and begin praying according to His will, we can be optimistic and confident about the outcome.

Whether your prayers have been positively answered, you are still awaiting an answer, or you have received a definite "No" to your request(s), be assured that God has His reasons for everything. Perhaps the analogy of Wilbur's unsuccessful "prayers" will help you as it did me, reminding you to remain faithful in God and His knowledge of what's best for you whenever your faith is tested. I believe that if we follow God's guidelines concerning prayer and stay focused on Him, we'll find contentment and peace in our prayer lives, no matter how our prayers are answered.

I want to conclude this chapter with the prayer our Master taught us ...

Our Father in heaven,
Hallowed be Your name.
Your Kingdom come.
Your will be done
On earth as *it is* in heaven.
Give us this day our daily bread.
And forgive us our debts,
As we forgive our debtors.
And do not lead us into temptation,
But deliver us from the evil one.
For Yours is the Kingdom and the power and the
glory forever.

Amen (Matthew 6:9-13, NKJV).

CHAPTER 7: DOWN TO THE BONES

One particular day, something out of the ordinary happened when I stooped down to take Wilbur's well-chewed rawhide bone away ... He growled at me! I realize that growling isn't unusual for most dogs, especially when they feel threatened, but Wilbur had never growled at me before that day. Unfortunately, it's now unusual for him *not* to growl at me when I have to take a bone away from him (which I must do to prevent him from choking). But the first time he did this, I was both surprised and irritated.

My feelings were certainly hurt and "my feathers were ruffled" by Wilbur's threatening growl. I felt that since *I* was the one who gave him the bone to enjoy in the first place, I was entitled to take the bone away without being threatened or "talked back to." However, after I analyzed my thoughts and feelings regarding Wilbur's behavior, I realized that I had no right to hold anything against him for growling at me because I, too, had "growled" many times in my life when things were taken from me. As a child, I would get angry and sulk when my parents grounded me from the television, telephone, or other privileges they had made possible for me to enjoy. Likewise, there have been times when God allowed something to be taken away from me, and I have grumbled at Him about my loss.

I thought about the biblical figure, Job, as I reflected upon these things. Most Christians are familiar with the story of Job—how Satan got permission from God to test him, sure that this righteous man would denounce his faith after experiencing tragedy. I can't imagine how devastated and hopeless Job must have felt as practically everything he valued was stripped away from him. In just one day, he lost his livestock, his servants, and all of his children. In spite of his losses, however, the first chapter of Job tells us this:

> Job got up and tore his robe and shaved his head. Then he fell to the ground in worship and said: "Naked I came from my mother's womb, and naked I will depart. The LORD gave and the LORD has taken away; may the name of the LORD be praised." In all this, Job did not sin by charging God with wrongdoing (Job 1:20-22).

Wow! What an incredible man! He lost so much, so quickly, yet he continued to praise God. Job's misfortunes didn't end there, however. The Bible tells us that his trials and tribulations continued. But he never cursed God or denounced his faith. The basis of Job's philosophy was simple: God gave him the things in his life, so He had the right to take them away. Job's reasoning was correct. He came into this world with nothing; therefore, nothing really belonged to him.

Of course, this is true for all of us. We don't truly own anything because everything we have comes from the hands of God. At some point or another, most of us have been guilty of living our lives and viewing our possessions as if they belong solely to us. If anyone or anything impedes our plans or desires, we all have been guilty of "growling." However, we must remember that God didn't have to give us anything—not even our very lives. When hardships and losses come our way, we must remember who is God, and we must be willing to accept that for reasons known only to Him, He gives *and* takes away.

◦━━━◦

Consolations

I have learned that Wilbur appreciates a good trade for his bones. Carrots are another favorite treat, so when I need to take a bone away from him, I've been giving him a carrot in its place. This strategy has made things easier for both Wilbur and me. I no longer have to deal with him growling at me, and I believe he feels compensated for the loss of his bone as he enjoys his carrot.

One day, as I made this common exchange with Wilbur, it occurred to me that God has done this type of thing for me as well. When I look back at the times when God allowed something to be taken from me or when I surrendered something to Him, I can see ways in which He blessed me in return. Sometimes God has given me double for my trouble, as the cliché goes; at the very least, He has given me revelations or blessings that helped make the transitions in my life smoother. Perhaps you have seen God work this way in your life.

God promises to work all things out for our good when we are devoted to Him (Romans 8:28). If you are familiar with how the book of Job ends, you know that God rewarded Job for his outstanding faithfulness. Job 42 states that God restored Job's fortunes "and gave him twice as much as he had before" (verse 10), and He "blessed the latter part of Job's life more than the former part" (verse 12). I'm sure that the loved ones Job lost were irreplaceable and greatly missed, but God blessed Job with an even larger family the second go-round. The latter blessings God bestowed upon Job certainly brought him joy and helped ease the pain of his losses.

I believe the story of Job perfectly illustrates how God compensates His children for their losses. Just as I replace Wilbur's bones with carrots, and just as many of you do similar things for your pets and/or children, God reimburses us for the things we must give up—whether it's now or when we get to Heaven. He never fails those who love and trust Him. For as long as we live here on earth, we will have to let go of things and people that we don't want to let go of, but we can be assured that our loving Master has a few "carrots" up His sleeve!

"Treats" That Steal Our Joy

By observing Wilbur with his bones, I've learned that hiding a bone can be a stressful dilemma for dogs! When I give Wilbur a rawhide bone, he normally goes straight into our carpeted bedroom and begins chewing it. But once in a while, his doggie instincts kick into high gear and he feels the need to hide it. Finding a safe hiding place isn't always easy though, so occasionally Wilbur paces the floor with a new bone in his mouth, whining and fretting as if he's terribly stressed. In these moments, I usually find myself wishing I had never given him the bone in the first place since it seems more like a burden than a treat. I myself feel stressed out just watching him!

Once, as I watched Wilbur fret over hiding a bone, I saw another parallel between his behavior and mine. Like Wilbur, I can sometimes be so consumed with my blessings that they begin to weigh me down. Consider the luxuries we enjoy here in the United States. Many amenities of modern life, such as nice homes, cars, and hot tubs, are unimaginable in other parts of the world. Many of us are blessed to have these luxuries, yet they can become financially, physically, and emotionally draining at times due to the energy and effort required to maintain them. Though we think they'll make us happier, the material things we wish for can actually become stumbling blocks that detract from our happiness.

I believe God has designed us to feel an emptiness in our hearts that only He can fill. When people start accumulating wealth and material possessions that consume their lives, the "hole" inside them often grows larger because they have less time to fill it with the genuine and lasting pleasures of God. There have been times in my life when I've been so consumed with *things*, such as finding the perfect curtains for my bedroom or the perfect dress to wear to a wedding, that I neglected to give God or the people in my life the attention they deserved. Does any of this sound familiar? I believe God often chooses not to give us some of the material things we desire (and takes some of them away) because He wants us to seek joy in having meaningful relationships with Him and others, and He knows how easily we are distracted by material possessions.

Balanced Blessings

On the flip side of the coin, I received another (very different) insight from observing Wilbur during the times when he seemed stressed over hiding a bone. I felt like God spoke to my heart, saying, *"See, when I choose to bless you, I want you to enjoy the blessings!"* Just as it bothers me to see Wilbur turn a treat into a stressful dilemma, I'm sure God doesn't like it when we turn His blessings into burdens or when we don't experience the joy He intended for us to get from them.

Have you ever met someone who seemed too humble? Is that even possible? I think it may be. Humility is a wonderful quality to have, no doubt, but sometimes I think too much of it can interfere with God's plans. For instance, some people never seem to give themselves any credit, and they don't feel they deserve anything good.

If you happen to be one of these people, I hope you will begin to accept and savor the blessings in your life, for "every good and perfect gift is from above, coming down from the Father of the heavenly lights ..." (James 1:17). The next time you receive an unexpected blessing from God, perhaps a gift or compliment from another person, give thanks and then enjoy it! I know it can be difficult not to feel guilty for our material blessings, especially when we see the depravity in the world around us. Certainly, God expects us to have compassion for others and give from our overabundance. However, this doesn't mean you should feel guilty when God gives you a gift because there are particular blessings that God wants *you* to be the sole recipient of.

I think I've learned some valuable lessons from observing Wilbur with his bones. I can clearly see that it's important for us to find a point of moderation when it comes to the blessings in our lives. I believe we should sometimes relax and experience the intended enjoyment from the "bones" our Master gives us (without being preoccupied by them); however, if our "bones" get taken away, we must remember that God was the one who gave them to us in the first place. When God decides to allow something or someone to be taken away from us, we would be wise not to "growl" at Him. Instead, we should trust Him and seek His "carrots" of consolation.

CHAPTER 8: TAKE YOUR CHANCES

I have already mentioned Wilbur's nosiness and how much trouble that characteristic can cause. One time, it nearly cost him his life ...

It was a cold December day, and I had just finished having Wilbur's nails trimmed—a task he doesn't allow my husband or me to do. Before returning home, I decided to stop in and visit with my grandparents while warming up by their fireplace. Since we live near them, Wilbur often joins me at their house and seems to enjoy visiting with "Granny" and "Papaw."

At some point during this particular visit, I realized I had not seen Wilbur for a few minutes. So I went to look for him and made a terrifying discovery. As I walked into my grandparents' laundry room, I saw an open closet door (which is normally closed), and just inside of it stood Wilbur, scarfing down rat poison! I was momentarily stunned and frozen with fear. However, since Wilbur was no stranger to emergencies, I knew exactly what to do and acted quickly.

Within three minutes, I had him home. I found the hydrogen peroxide (to induce vomiting), squirted it down Wilbur's throat via a syringe at record speed, and prayed for God to spare his life. The stakes had never been this high before, and I was seriously scared I might lose him. Thankfully, the poison came out of his system in no time, and I felt a huge sense of relief, knowing he was probably going to be okay.

I then called the vet, who told me to bring Wilbur in right away for an examination. Frightened by the urgency of the vet technician's tone (even after I told her that Wilbur had thrown up all the poison), I rushed him there as quickly as possible. During the entire drive to the vet's office, I reflected on some of my wonderful memories with Wilbur and earnestly prayed for his life.

After performing an exam, the vet gave me some good news—praise the Lord! He said I had done a good job of quickly taking charge of the situation and that Wilbur would probably not have any complications from this dangerous ordeal. As a precaution, the vet prescribed some Vitamin K tablets for him to take for a month, just in case any of the poison had entered his system. But, thankfully, everything appeared to be just fine.

Needless to say, this experience really shook me up. If I hadn't caught Wilbur in the act, he probably would've bled to death in the days that followed. Even more frightening is that we probably wouldn't have known anything was wrong with him until it was too late—we would've just walked into the house and found him dead. Although Wilbur had some pretty close calls before this one (he must have nine lives!), I had always pictured him living for many years, at least until his early teens. After this ordeal, however, reality confronted me head on, and my perspective of his life was changed. I realized that I couldn't even take my young Wilbur's life for granted, and I'm now more thankful than ever to have him and to receive his love and slobbery kisses every day!

For a Limited Time

This incident with Wilbur turned out well. But, unfortunately, we all know that many situations don't turn out this way. Doesn't it seem like the number of major tragedies in our nation and around the world is increasing exponentially? It seems like every time I turn on the news, there has been another natural disaster or worse, an act of terror. Lives are lost, people are injured, and each event seems so senseless. Unfortunately, due to the Bible's warning signs of the end times (see Matthew 24), I believe the number of evil acts and natural disasters will only increase.

I think it's important for us to remember that the only guarantees in life are the promises of God. We, or someone we love, can be taken from this life in the blink of an eye, whether due to a natural disaster, terrorist attack, accident, or illness. James 4:14 describes our temporary state in this way:

> Why, you do not even know what will happen tomor-
> row. What is your life? You are a mist that appears for
> a little while and then vanishes.

Simply put, our tomorrow or the tomorrow of a loved one may never come.

This is a harsh reality, and I'm sure many of you have experienced it firsthand. We usually try not to think about the uncertainties of life because they are disturbing and scary; however, it's important to be aware of just how sacred and fragile life is. I don't know about you, but I often get so wrapped up in my busy, day-to-day life that I lose sight of what's most important.

Every now and then, I'll get a call from a loved one and huff out loud when I recognize their phone number on caller ID because I'm just not in the mood to talk. Too many times I have been sitting on the couch when my husband arrives home from work, and I just barely acknowledge him with a less-than-enthusiastic, "Hey, how was your day?" Wilbur, on the other hand, is jumping up and down, looking out the window, barking, and wagging his tail as if it's been a year since he last saw him! He certainly knows how to welcome my husband and me, making us feel special every single time we arrive home, and I know his method of greeting is much better than my own.

I can't help but feel shallow when I ask myself, *What if this were the last night I had the chance to greet my husband?* If I knew it would be the last time, I surely wouldn't sit on the couch focusing on other things. Instead, I would act a lot like Wilbur; I would jump up, open the door, and greet my husband with a big hug and kiss. I'm also ashamed when I consider the way I sometimes feel when someone calls me and I'm not in the mood to talk. I ask myself, *What if that was the last conversation I ever had with that person?* Talk about regrets!

I think it's safe to say that most of the time we don't make a huge spectacle over seeing or talking with family and friends that we communicate with on a regular basis. Unless we know that someone is deathly ill, we usually take for granted that we'll have more time to spend with them. Am I right? In today's culture, it just doesn't seem "cool" for us to get all mushy with those we frequently see. If it's a special occasion, we may get sentimental and share with someone just how much they mean to us, but it generally isn't the norm. I believe it should be.

Considering Wilbur's close call and the tragedies I often hear about, I believe I should be more joyful toward my loved ones and appreciate every moment I have with them. We just never know when our last chance will be to make a huge spectacle over someone we love. Life is precious, so like Wilbur (and dogs in general), we should take every opportunity we have to show and tell those we love just how much they mean to us.

ADDENDUM

The inspiration for me to write this chapter came just after the Colorado movie theatre massacre. Twelve people lost their lives in an instant in that tragedy. Many others were physically injured, and countless people experienced emotional injuries that will likely last a lifetime. Since the time I originally began this chapter, several other disturbing events have taken place. Rather than incorporating these occurrences into the original text, I have decided to tag them on in order to illustrate the unexpected "addendums" in life.

I doubt any of us will ever forget the terrible tragedy that took place the morning of December 14, 2012, at Sandy Hook Elementary School in Newtown, Connecticut. Twenty innocent children and six adult staff members were shot and killed in a brutal, senseless shooting rampage. I felt a knot in my stomach and cried as I watched the victims' pictures come across the television screen and heard some of their family members expressing their grief.

There are simply no words to describe this tragedy. I feared there would be more mass shootings after the Colorado movie theatre massacre; however, I never fathomed someone would be overcome with enough evil to target an elementary school! Sandy Hook serves as another sad reminder that life is extremely fragile. I'm sure there are many people who lost children or loved ones that day who wish they had a chance to relive the last encounter they had with that person … to hold them a little longer, to squeeze them a little tighter, and to look them deep in the eyes and tell them once more just how much they were loved. I'm sure none of these families expected *not* to have another chance to do those things. It's just so, so tragic.

A Close Call

About one month after the tragedy in Newtown, Connecticut, I was faced with the harsh possibility of losing my best friend, Maria. I'm still in shock about what happened to her as I write this …

Maria and I became best friends when we were in second grade. We were both only children, so we quickly became like sisters. We spent the night with each other nearly every Friday night for at least 10 years. We went on family and church trips together. We went to prom together … You get the picture. We were practically inseparable and even had our own secret sign language and special notebooks dedicated to communicating with one another. (We thought we were pretty slick, writing to one another during class while the teachers thought we were taking notes!) After high school, our lives went in different directions, but we always remained close at heart and continued to share some special, memorable times together. Maria is a wonderful friend who understands me like none other. She has always been a strong, reliable shoulder for me to cry on through the difficult times in my life.

Maria and I had always joked about how my life seemed so full of drama, especially when compared to hers. She was always healthy and "normal," whereas I had my share of issues and minor health ailments. But one day, out of the blue, things suddenly shifted, and Maria became the center of some major drama. I received the dreaded phone call—the kind I have always feared—and found out Maria had just had a stroke and was in the hospital! I know my jaw dropped and my mind clouded over as I sat down on the hearth of my fireplace, listening to the story unfold.

Maria had presented to the local emergency room with slurred speech, along with weakness and numbness in her right arm, hand, and leg. The doctor soon realized she had had a stroke, so he transferred her to a larger, more advanced hospital. As I was hearing about all of this, they were performing further tests to determine what was going on. Thankfully, Maria was still conscious and hadn't suffered any apparent problems with her memory or personality.

Surprisingly, I didn't immediately break down after receiving this devastating news, likely because I was in such a state of shock. There were just so many unanswered questions, and for a while, I felt like I was trying to make my way through a dense fog. All I knew was that my best friend, only 33 years old and in seemingly perfect health only a week before, had suffered a stroke. It was so unbelievable!

As a nurse, I was all too familiar with the grim possibilities. I remembered that a few weeks before, Maria had complained of having a bad headache that lasted an entire weekend, so I grew concerned that she may have a slow-leaking brain aneurysm. I was extremely scared because I knew if she had a brain aneurysm, things could get very serious, very fast, and she would definitely have to undergo brain surgery.

During the 30-minute drive to the hospital, I prayed diligently, nonstop. Once there, I found out Maria had internal tears in two of the major arteries that supply blood to the back of the brain (likely due to working out at the gym several days before). Blood clots had formed, broken loose, and dispersed throughout her brain, causing the stroke. The worst part was that she still had a large clot near her brainstem, the area that controls the essential functions for life including breathing and heart rate.

This news hit me like a ton of bricks, and all at once, I felt a sense of desperate urgency to see and talk with Maria. I felt pretty confident that I would get the chance to see her alive, but after hearing this news, I feared that I didn't have much time to see *her* again ... not the Maria I knew. I reached a breaking point and started crying and praying that, at the very least, I could see and talk with her one more time. Of course, I prayed that God would heal her completely, but I essentially *begged* Him to allow me the chance to say my goodbyes if it was her time to go. For as long as I live, I doubt I'll ever forget the helpless, gut-wrenching feeling I experienced during that time.

Thanks be to God, Maria has made a near-full recovery in a very short time. I truly consider it a miracle for her to be alive today and to have come out of this ordeal practically unscathed. I'm so grateful that God answered the many prayers for Maria's healing, and I cherish the blessing of her friendship now more than ever.

Loud and Clear

I had to include this addendum to emphasize how critical it is to let your loved ones know how much they mean to you and to make peace with them if there are unresolved issues. After coming close to losing my best friend, I've learned some valuable lessons. Things could have easily turned out much differently, and I got a glimpse of what it would be like to have regrets for not making every minute count. None of us like the idea of people thinking we are overly emotional or crazy, but there were some moments during this life-or-death situation when I regretted *not* being more crazy—crazy over Maria!

During the uncertain moments, I remember wishing I could relive my last encounter with her or just add one minute of time to that encounter to express my love for her. I realized how much more at peace I would've felt in that hospital waiting room if I had recently said something to her like, "You know, you're like a sister to me, and I'm so blessed to have you in my life. Don't ever forget that I love you." It wouldn't have changed the harsh reality I faced of potentially losing her, but at least I could've been standing on the edge of uncertainty knowing without a doubt that Maria knew how much she meant to me. Yes, it may have seemed a little strange (for both Maria and I) if I had added some sentimental words to the end of our usual weekly telephone conversation. But so what? At least I wouldn't have had any regrets for *not* doing that.

Many people live with regrets for not expressing their feelings to a loved one before it was too late, and this is a difficult and touchy subject for all of us. I know it's easy to take people for granted. As a result of my experiences, I'm seeking to do better in this respect ... to be more thankful for the special people (and pet) God has placed in my life and to cherish the times I have with them. But I still have room for improvement. May we all be reminded of the importance of making every moment count each time we are greeted with joy and excitement by our dogs. In many ways, I honestly believe they're smarter than we are! They show us that it's good to be a little fanatical over those we love. I pray you will never hesitate to share your love for people just because you're scared they will think you're an overemotional sap. Live and love in ways you'll never have to regret—even if you have to bark, run around in circles, and wag your tail!

CHAPTER 9: UNCONTAINABLE JOY

Wilbur's enthusiasm over me returning home gives me something to look forward to each day. As I discussed in the previous chapter, Wilbur's way of greeting and welcoming my husband and me is a wonderful example of how we should make a big deal over our loved ones every time we get the chance. His habitual display of joy and excitement when we arrive home also led me to question myself, *How often do I get that excited to be with my Master?* One day while enjoying Wilbur's warm welcome, I realized that I am seldom that enthusiastic about being in God's presence.

The times that I have fully acknowledged and appreciated God's presence have been amazing experiences in my life. There have been several times when I have felt His nearness and acted much as Wilbur does when he greets me. During those times, God's presence was practically tangible, and I felt an indescribable sense of joy, wonder, love, and peace overflowing in my heart and soul. I couldn't help but cry tears of joy and raise my arms up in the air, praising God.

As I experienced these close encounters with God, I felt like all my walls came crashing down, releasing a flood of emotions that had been bottled up inside of me. Twice, I've experienced my left leg jerking uncontrollably for whatever reason—as if my physical body was so overcome with the presence of God that I lost control. If you've ever experienced this type of encounter with God, I'm sure you will agree that it's the most wonderful feeling ever. It's such a privilege to feel so close to the God of the universe—to know that the One who hung the moon and stars cares enough about measly me to make such a grand entrance into my house!

Anytime, Anywhere

Thankfully, unlike Wilbur, I never have to wait around for my Master to show up. Many times I don't feel like God is close by, but since I'm a believer, His Holy Spirit is actually *inside* of me at all times (see 1 Corinthians 6:19). Isn't that amazing? The Bible tells us to "Draw near to God and He will draw near to you" (James 4:8, NKJV). I have certainly found this Scripture to be true. Any time that I've whole-heartedly sought after God, He has made His closeness to me very apparent.

There have been a few times in my life when I was completely astounded by the sense of God's presence. One night before falling asleep, I prayed a heartfelt prayer through my tears, and later that night I awoke to the sound of my music box playing! I completely froze in fear for a few seconds, and the music stopped playing. Then before I could even process what had just happened, the music box started playing again. I felt a supernatural presence in the room, and when I mustered enough courage to slowly roll over and look in the direction of the music box, I just knew I was about to see an angelic figure. I actually didn't see anything, but the music stopped and started once again, so I pinched myself to make sure I wasn't dream-ing! Of course, there's no logical explanation for how or why a music box would play *three* separate times independent of human interven-tion. I believe it was God (the Father, Son, and Holy Spirit), giving me confirmation in the physical realm that He is always with me and is attentive to my prayers.

Even though physical encounters with God are the exception rather than the rule, I have intensely felt His presence many times during prayer and while listening to Christian music. Sometimes when I'm down, confused, or simply longing to feel closer to God, I'll turn on some Christian music or play hymns on my piano and sing. Other times, I'll sit on my back deck and pray as I admire His creation. Regardless of where I am or how bad my singing may be, God has never failed to assure me that He's there.

Stop to Smell His Roses

I easily become overwhelmed with a sense of wonder and awe when I observe the fascinating things God has created and contemplate how great He must be. When I sit outside on a clear night and look at the multitude of stars stretched across the sky, I experience a powerful connection with the Master Artist. I know that I could experience so much more joy and peace in my life if only I took the time to soak in His presence and celebrate how wonderful He is. But instead, I typically go through my daily routine in my own little bubble, too busy or caught up in myself to let Him really saturate my life. Sadly, I believe this is very common among Christians. Our Master is always there, waiting on us to acknowledge Him and be filled with an abundance of joy and peace, but we often walk right past the opportunities to genuinely experience Him.

I have found that the days I spend time with God and His Word first thing in the morning (even if it's only a few minutes) go much more smoothly—my attitude and whole outlook on life is changed for the better. An unexplainable feeling of calm assurance comes over me, and I'm much better equipped to handle the challenges of life. Also, when I take time to read the Bible at bedtime, I'm able to reprocess everything that occurred during the day and feel emotionally and spiritually restored. Therefore, it makes no sense for me (or any other Christian) to pass up the blessings of love, joy, and peace which come from simply delighting in God's presence.

I believe most of us could benefit from taking a lesson from our dogs and being more excited to encounter our Master. Each morning when we rise, we should be happy to know that He's with us and enjoy spending some quality time with Him. Don't you know it brings much pleasure to the heart of God when we simply want to just be with Him? He probably experiences the same, warm feeling we get when our pets or children curl up next to us, simply desiring to be close. I think if we make a point to be more aware of our Master's presence in our daily lives, we will bring Him glory and oftentimes find ourselves running around, "barking" shouts of uncontainable joy!

Spirit and Truth

While on the subject of being joyful in God's presence, I'd like to say some things regarding public praise and worship. The freedom to praise God in public is a great privilege. It's so nice to be able to fellowship with our brothers and sisters in Christ and to support, encourage, and pray for one another. People attend church for various reasons, but the main purpose of church is to unite believers. It gives us an opportunity to formally acknowledge God's goodness and power and to worship Him together.

Sadly, though, I must admit that many times I've gone to church simply because I've felt like I *ought* to ... It's Sunday and I'm a Christian, so I should go. Also, I've often gone to church for a pick-me-up because I was in a slump and desperately needed some spiritual refreshment. In other words, many times I've not gone to church with the primary intent of worshiping God. On more than one occasion, I have sat in church like the proverbial "knot on a log," pondering the problems in my life—even as the praise team sang with enthusiasm and waved their arms in the air.

I believe Psalm 100 gives us the perfect illustration of what worship should be. It states:

> Worship the Lord with *gladness*;
> come before him with *joyful songs.*
> Know that the Lord is God.
> It is he who made us, and we are his;
> we are his people, the sheep of his pasture.
>
> Enter his gates with *thanksgiving*
> and his courts with *praise;*
> give thanks to him and praise his name
> (Psalm 100: 2-4, emphasis mine).

Unfortunately, there are many Christians, including some of you, who are in the same boat that I'm in—we fall very short of worshiping God according to Psalm 100. There's another important Scripture regarding worship that I often fail to achieve:

> God is spirit, and his worshipers must worship in the
> Spirit and in truth (John 4:24).

I must admit that there have been times when I have avoided pouring out my spirit and true self to God in front of others because I was scared they would think I was crazy or fanatical. One very memorable example of this was when I attended a Beth Moore event at a large local coliseum. I felt like the presence of the Holy Spirit was practically tangible as thousands of women were standing and singing the familiar hymn, "On Christ, The Solid Rock I Stand." I felt the sting of tears filling my eyes, and suddenly I needed to lift my hands up to God and let the flood of tears flow. Just as quickly, though, I thought of my mom and aunt who were standing beside me. I had never seen either of them get physically involved in worship, and I felt my flesh screaming out, *You better not embarrass yourself!*

My spirit was completely opposed to my flesh in that moment (though it always is, according to Galatians 5:17), and I felt a major tug-of-war going on inside me. Sadly, as in many cases, my flesh won out ... I tried desperately to conceal my tears and to downplay my emotions. (Believe me, with the overwhelming sense of the Holy Spirit within that coliseum, this was a huge struggle.) I eventually felt the tears subside, and when I glanced over at my mom and aunt, I realized that they, too, had tears in their eyes and were fanning their faces. I believe my mom said something like, "Whew! You can really feel the Spirit moving!" I nodded my head in agreement and thought, *Wow, I'm glad I'm not the only one!* I got the feeling that my mom and aunt were thinking the same thing, too.

Regretfully, this wasn't the first or last time I have experienced this type of battle during public worship. Have you ever experienced times in church when your soul cried out to worship God with physical expression, yet your human nature stepped in and restrained you from drawing attention to yourself? I imagine this is quite common among believers because none of us like to appear vulnerable or overly emotional. We all want to look our best in front of others, as if we are completely put together with everything under control ... Heaven forbid we remove our masks and let people have a look at our real, flawed selves—or get carried away with joy (like our dogs) in the presence of our Master and risk being viewed as fanatical or crazy!

In 1 Thessalonians 5:19, Paul writes, "Do not quench the Spirit." In other words, don't put out the fire God has started within you. But that's exactly what I have done many times, simply because I was too prideful to allow myself to appear out of control or vulnerable in front of others. I'm saddened and ashamed to know that I've often failed to worship God with my true spirit and, therefore, limited the power of the Holy Spirit to move through me and possibly others as well. I've grown in this respect, but I still have a ways to go.

———

Conducive Places

One significant factor that influences how we worship God is the church we attend. Though the Bible makes it clear that we are all part of one body—the body of Christ—the fact remains that there are numerous denominations within the body of Christ. These denominations often differ in their worship practices, as do individual churches within each denomination.

Without a doubt, the atmosphere in some churches is much more conducive to worshiping in spirit and in truth than other churches. My earliest years were spent in a Lutheran church, and our services were very orderly and formal. I never heard a person shout an "Amen" or "Hallelujah," nor did I ever see people lifting their hands during worship. So the first time I attended a Baptist church, I experienced a bit of culture shock! Although I would never trade my early experiences in the small, close-knit church my family attended, I soon found that the more open style of worship seemed more authentic and better suited to my worship preferences.

One day at work, my supervisor and I had a conversation about different types of churches. She told me that she attended a "Holy Ghost-filled church," which she said was technically an Apostolic church. I was unfamiliar with either of these terms. Perhaps some of you are familiar with or attend this type of church, but I was clueless. By my supervisor's description, this type of church is very lively and enthusiastic, and some members of the congregation speak in and interpret tongues.

I had never heard someone speak in tongues before, which actually concerned me a little. Although speaking in tongues was not part of my faith tradition, I knew the practice was mentioned in the Bible.

My childhood church recognized Pentecost—an observance of the events that took place in the second chapter of Acts when Peter and many others were filled with the Holy Spirit and spoke in tongues. This bit of knowledge made the practice intriguing, and I figured that attending my supervisor's church would be the perfect opportunity for me to expand my horizons.

So several weeks after our conversation, my husband and I attended her church and had a "Wow!" experience. Everyone there was so warm and inviting, and practically all of them were smiling and radiating a sense of gladness and deep joy. The atmosphere was unlike that of any other church I had ever attended. I noticed a few people mumbling in tongues during one of the prayers, and one lady jogged for joy around the isles with a big smile on her face during one of the praise songs. Although these behaviors were certainly unusual to me, I didn't feel uncomfortable because nothing about their worship appeared fake, irreverent, or simply for show. I actually felt quite comfortable and at peace among this congregation.

I definitely sensed an unbound presence of the Holy Spirit in that church, and the atmosphere felt so alive and refreshing. People seemed to be genuinely praising God from the depths of their hearts and souls, and it was nice to feel "normal" when I raised my hands in praise. I was encouraged knowing that I wouldn't have been out of place if I had shouted "Hallelujah" or "Amen!" It didn't feel like the Holy Spirit was on a leash, so to speak, so God was being fully worshiped and praised. It was great to witness believers displaying physical excitement and joy when in the presence of their Master ... just like my sweet Wilbur!

It perplexes and saddens me that in the majority of churches today, there are unspoken traditions that discourage people from worshiping God in spirit, truth, and in accordance with Psalm 100. I realize that there's a fine line in maintaining reverence and order in church while displaying joy and genuineness at the same time. But I believe above all else, God desires for His children to join together and *joyfully* praise Him.

God is so deserving of sincere worship, and we are meant to feel the reality and power of His presence when we worship Him. Most of us could and should get a little more excited in church. Take it from a nurse with more than a decade of experience—we are all broken and crazy in some way or another; we're all in desperate need of God. So don't shortchange God and yourself by not being authentic and joyful during worship because of the fear of what others may think of you. Keep in mind that worship is all about giving God glory—not about trying to preserve your own.

Whether we are alone or with a multitude of believers, we should frequently acknowledge and celebrate God. It's amazing that my little dachshund reinforced to me such an important, yet basic, spiritual truth ... We can and should take advantage of the gift of our Master's presence anywhere and everywhere, and we should never withhold our genuine and joyful shouts of praise!

CHAPTER 10: COLORBLIND

I looked around as I sat among a circle of about 20 people. There were men and women of different races, sizes, and ages all around me. They were wearing different types of clothing and appeared to come from different classes of society. *Different*—that's the key word.

One African American man evoked a sense of fear in me; I surely wouldn't have wanted to encounter him in a dark alley—nor the young white man with multiple tattoos on his huge biceps. Next to me sat an older woman who was rather unkempt, and I pictured her standing in line at the homeless shelter.

Across from me, there was a thin woman in rather skimpy clothing, and I figured she may have hung out on the streets. However, the man wearing designer clothing and glasses appeared to be on the opposite end of the social spectrum. He was middle-aged and graying just a tad near his temples, giving him a distinguished look, and I assumed he was a wealthy lawyer or banker.

Almost directly in front of me I saw a heavy, older lady wearing a multi-colored housecoat, and I automatically imagined her being like Madea—the outspoken, audacious movie character that my husband and I get a kick out of watching. Beside her, there was a man who appeared mentally ill, rocking back and forth in his chair. Then there was another woman who looked like a "cat lady" to me ... you know, the lady who's never married and lives with 20 cats. (Before you label me as prejudiced, please keep reading—you'll understand more on the following pages.)

I felt a little uncomfortable sitting among this group of people because I didn't know any of them, except for an acquaintance who was sitting next to me. He was a counselor in this place—in the inpatient psychiatric unit where I was assisting with a group therapy session. And guess who else was assisting? I'll give you a hint … he was "praying" in the middle of the circle, getting showered with "Oohs," "Ahhs," and laughter! Yes, Wilbur was once a therapy dog.

Though never trained or specially certified, Wilbur met the criteria to be a part of the pet therapy program at the hospital where I once worked. I knew he would be great at making patients smile, so I signed us up to volunteer for a few hours every other week. The 30-minute ride was quite long for Wilbur, but he seemed excited when he pranced onto the hospital elevator. He proudly sported his UNC Tar Heels collar and leash, and he even had his own photo name badge! You could barely see him in the photo because he is so black, but I thought it was precious.

Our first stop was the psychiatric unit, where I observed the people I described above. Wilbur was supposed to be a source of comfort and entertainment for the patients, and for the most part, he fulfilled his purpose. I took his ball so he could play with the patients, and I also brought some treats to coax him into "praying." He didn't perform under pressure as well as I had hoped, but he did "pray" a little for the patients, and they seemed to thoroughly enjoy that.

Wilbur brought forth smiles on every face, just as I had anticipated. Most everyone held out their hands, wanting to pet him, and he made his way around the circle, briefly sniffing and greeting everyone. I noticed that he did not "judge" anyone. He seemed oblivious to the differences among the people in the room and treated everyone the same. They say that dogs are colorblind. I don't know if I completely believe that, but in regards to prejudices or discrimination, I know this has to be true.

I couldn't help but think that Wilbur's behavior and interaction with this group of people was the perfect illustration of how Christian people should be. He was doing exactly what God calls His children to do; he judged no one and was friendly to all. I believe that most of the strangers we encounter, regardless of their outer appearances, have some tenderness within and want to love and to be loved. And as God's children, He expects us to extend a loving, accepting attitude toward everyone. Of course, as with most anything, there are some exceptions to this. God gave us the sense of fear for a reason, and we should pay attention to any legitimate fears we have concerning others in order to stay safe.

To have a functional society, we certainly need laws, a judicial system, and formal punishment for lawbreakers; but we must remember that only God, who knows all things, has the right to truly judge someone and their character. I love the story in John 8 where Jesus tells the people who are getting ready to stone an adulterous woman, "Let any one of you who is without sin be the first to throw a stone at her" (verse 7). And when everyone left and no one was there to condemn her, Jesus told the woman, "… neither do I condemn you … Go now and leave your life of sin" (John 8:11).

This story emphasizes that all people are sinful. We each know within our hearts that we are in no position to judge others because we fall very short of the mark ourselves. In this discriminating and judgmental world we live in, I believe it's very important that Christians set the example of displaying unconditional love and respect to others. We should never come across as "holier-than-thou"-type people who make unbelievers feel like they must be perfect to follow Christ.

I'm not saying that Christians should condone fornication, adultery, homosexuality, drug abuse, idolatry, or any other sin. God has said in His Word that these things are wrong, and we must acknowledge and uphold *His* stance on such sins. But since we are all sinners, redeemed only through the grace of God, we need to share the truth of God's standards to other people in a loving, nonjudgmental way.

83

I believe we can disapprove of the sin, yet love and show love to the sinner, simultaneously.

———

Corrective Lenses

I typically have no problem extending love and friendship to others, regardless of their appearances or lifestyles. It has never been my nature to be condescending or discriminating. When it comes to valuing and loving others, I can honestly say that I have always been "colorblind." However, I must admit that I have a tendency (as I believe most all of us do) to stereotype people—to assume certain things about them based on the way they dress, talk, or wear their hair. This is what I intended to illustrate to you by describing the different people in the therapy group. Those descriptions include some uncomfortable stereotypes, and I recognize that I often recall those stereotypes in my initial perceptions of people, despite my efforts to be nonjudgmental.

Unfortunately, I don't believe it's possible for anyone to look through untainted lenses, completely free of stereotypes and assumptions. We simply don't have that much control over the thoughts that pop into our minds. However, I do believe we can be more aware of the perceptions we have of people and realize that they are just that—*perceptions,* not reality.

I think most of us consider ourselves good judges of character. We tend to think we have people figured out from the first time we meet them, right? I don't think we realize how often we place people in undeserved categories. I believe we should make a conscious effort to avoid doing this; there are just too many things about every person that do not meet the eye. We are often mistaken when we try to classify people without getting to know them first.

Several past teachers and professors had a saying about assumptions that I have found to be absolutely true. I'm sure many of you have also heard this said: Take a good look at the word *assume*. Notice that you can break the word down into three smaller words or parts—*ass*, *u*, and *me* ... Hence, assuming makes an ass of you and me! I have never forgotten this clever insight, and unfortunately, I've discovered the truth in it the hard way a few times. In my nursing career I have learned never to assume that the person sitting beside one of my elderly patients is a son or daughter. A few times, I have wrongly assumed that a spouse was a child, causing some very uncomfortable moments! There are times when just a simple question can prevent a lot of embarrassment and awkwardness.

I have learned that assuming is a form of judgment that can be destructive, even when there's no evil intent involved. Assumptions inevitably affect how we relate to other people and how they relate to us. For example, I feel like some people assume the reason why my husband and I haven't had children is because we either can't have them or because we're too selfish to have them. Neither of these reasons is true, yet if someone has such assumptions, it's impossible for their thoughts, feelings, and actions toward us not to be affected by these flawed beliefs.

Unfortunately, I believe we have all been affected by people assuming untrue things about us, and we have all affected other people by assuming wrong things about them. In the courtroom of life, I think we have all alternately played the judge and the defendant. This is just part of being human. However, God's Word gives us instruction regarding judgment and discrimination that we would be wise to heed. Matthew 7:2 warns:

> For in the same way you judge others, you will be judged, and with the measure you use, it will be measured to you.

I don't know about you, but I want to be judged as leniently as possible. So I try my best not to judge others … That's some serious business!

The Bible says that showing favoritism is also a sin (see James 2:9) and that "God does not show favoritism" (Acts 10:34). He "does not look at the things people look at. People look at the outward appearance, but the Lord looks at the heart" (1 Samuel 16:7). Human beings are made in the image of God, but when it comes to looking past exterior appearances, dogs are much greater imitators of Him than we are. A dog couldn't care less about a person's appearance, so long as they don't feel threatened. Dogs would just as soon snuggle up to a sweaty, over-weight man as they would a movie star wearing Calvin Klein cologne!

In a world that's obsessed with appearances, it's nice to know that we can count on God and dogs to look past the exterior and into the hearts of men … to look for and value inner beauty. The Bible says that we should live like "there is no longer Jew or Gentile, slave or free, male and female" because we "are all one in Christ Jesus" (Galatians 3:28, NLT). So please join me in trying to imitate Wilbur among that circle of people, extending friendliness and love to all those we encounter, regardless of appearances and social statuses. In doing so, we can be vessels of Christ's unconditional love in a world that so desperately needs it.

CHAPTER 11: FEARLESS

Wilbur's time as a therapy dog was brief, but only because of my limitations, not his. Our volunteer work included visiting patients in the Cancer Center after our participation in the psychiatric group therapy. This meant I had to hold and carry Wilbur a lot when making our rounds to see the cancer patients, and my fragile shoulders started acting up because of this. After a few steroid injections in my shoulders, I decided it was best to give up the pet therapy volunteer work.

In the short while that Wilbur and I visited patients in the cancer unit, however, Wilbur managed to teach me another valuable lesson—one that I believe came from the heart of God. As we made our rounds to visit the cancer patients, I noticed that Wilbur greeted everyone in a consistent manner, even though there were some obvious differences among them (just as in the psychiatric unit). He was just as excited to get close to and "kiss" the sickly, disheveled-looking patients as he was the ones who had no apparent signs of sickness. I, on the other hand, must admit that I was reluctant to get as close to the patients with IV transfusions, suction tubing, catheters, and other medical devices; although my apprehension had nothing to do with the people directly.

Since taking Microbiology in college, I'm quite the "germaphobe." Of course, hospitals are a challenge for people like me because everyone knows they are full of nasty germs. Bacteria and viruses lurk around everywhere, especially in and around patients' wounds and such. You're probably wondering why and how I became a nurse … Well, when I'm at work, I typically don't worry too much about germs because I can simply put on a pair of gloves when I'm around patients. Many times, I put on a pair of gloves if I'm going to be touching anything in a patient's vicinity—not just when I know I'm going to be in contact with bodily fluids (as is standard). And when I know a patient has an infection or a blood-borne disease, I put on gloves before I even walk into their room!

That may seem a little extreme, but it helps put my mind at ease. It's very common for me to have dry, cracked skin due to the amount of times I'm required to wash my hands, so this causes me more paranoia. Therefore, I think it's best for me to just put on gloves when I feel uncomfortable so that I can focus on my patients rather than on the germs or substances I may be getting on my hands. But in this new volunteer role I found myself in, it just didn't seem right for me to put on gloves when visiting the patients, especially since they seemed happy and eager to lay their hands on my unsanitary dog who could spread germs to them!

So I was definitely out of my comfort zone in this situation. I cringed on the inside when I saw Wilbur approaching a Foley (urinary) catheter bag dangling from a bed and when a patient stroked Wilbur's head after just laying down a freshly used Kleenex! (I'm fairly certain most everyone would've felt the same.) But I was influenced by observing Wilbur's ability to get up close and personal with these patients and the germs that were likely surrounding them.

Of course, Wilbur knows nothing about diseases and germs, and I'm pretty sure there's *nothing* he considers to be gross based on the nasty things I've seen him do! But by watching him live out my fears, so to speak, I realized that my fears were pretty unfounded and irrelevant in the grand scheme of things. I mean, Wilbur brought forth so much joy and many much-needed smiles, and nothing bad happened as a result of him being touched by those hands which had just put down a dirty Kleenex. So this uncomfortable experience actually ended up bringing me revelation and a sense of freedom.

———

No Holding Back

Watching Wilbur get up close and personal with everyone, with no regard for germs and such, showed me how God intends for me to be. Through this experience, I realized just how fearful, selfish, and guarded I can be sometimes. More importantly, I saw how these qualities can hinder me from fulfilling God's purposes.

The Bible states: "For God has not given us a spirit of fear, but of power and of love and of a sound mind" (2 Timothy 1:7, NKJV). When you really stop and think about it, lingering fear is a lack of faith in God's provision. I also believe fear is sometimes rooted in selfishness, or at least in self-preservation. If I really want to be obedient to God's command of loving my neighbor as myself, I should be willing to push my fears and hang-ups aside on behalf of others.

Jesus didn't think too highly of Himself or allow fear to keep Him from touching "the unclean." It wasn't customary, nor even lawful, to touch people with leprosy in Jesus' day; yet Matthew 8 says:

> When Jesus came down from the mountainside, large crowds followed him. A man with leprosy came and knelt before him and said, "Lord, if you are willing, you can make me clean." Jesus reached out his hand and touched the man. "I am willing," he said. "Be clean!" Immediately he was cleansed of his leprosy (verses 1-3).

Jesus gave His disciples the following instructions in Matthew 10:

Go rather to the lost sheep of Israel. As you go, pro-
claim this message: "The kingdom of heaven has come
near." Heal the sick, raise the dead, cleanse those
who have leprosy, drive out demons. Freely you have
received; freely give (verses 6-8).

This instruction applies to followers of Christ today as well. As
Christians, we have been given the most valuable gift anyone can
receive, so God intends for us to freely give of ourselves. God calls us to
step out of our comfort zones—to let go of our selfishness and fears—
to serve others, even the outcasts of society. This means we have to
dive in and get our hands dirty sometimes. This may not be easy, but
the rewards are many and everlasting. Remember that, according to
Matthew 25:40, whatever you do for "the least of these," you do it unto
Christ Himself.

As I write this, I'm preparing to go on my first mission trip. I will
be chaperoning the youth of my church as they work in Puerto Rico.
Since I speak a moderate amount of Spanish, I may be able to help out
with translating as well. I have to admit that I'm not looking forward
to being without some of the physical comforts I have here at home.
We won't have air conditioning there, and I can't stand the heat. So
I'm sure I'll be absolutely miserable at times, especially considering the
fact that we'll be there the last week of June. Also, I'm concerned that
I won't be able to sleep well because I usually require complete silence
to fall asleep, and on the trip, I'll be sharing a room with many people.
Did I mention I'm afraid of snakes? (Really, really afraid!) Then there's
the concern I have of contracting food poisoning ... So, it's obvious that
in the fleshly, physical sense, I'm really dreading this trip!

However, I'm trying to push the negatives out of my mind and
focus on the spiritual side of things because I know that my soul,
which is my *true* self, will enjoy and prosper from this upcoming
experience. In the midst of the fears and physical discomforts I'm
sure to encounter, I know it's going to feel so good to be serving a

purpose much greater than myself, making a positive impact on many lives and for God's Kingdom. When I think about things from this perspective, I'm very excited to go experience what God has in store for me (and the others in my group). I've decided to put the lesson I have learned from watching Wilbur to good use—I'm going to cast my fears, selfishness, and quirks aside in order to extend the unconditional love of Christ.

Confidence to the Next Level

While on the topic of fear, I want to share another biblical insight I have gathered from watching Wilbur, and, in hindsight, from all of the dachshunds I've had. If you know anything about dachshunds, you know they can be ferocious little dogs! They were actually bred to hunt badgers, which are very vicious animals, so I guess this explains why dachshunds can be so brave and tenacious. It may surprise you (as it did me) to know that studies have shown that dachshunds are considered to be the most aggressive breed of dog in the world! They reportedly bite more than any other breed.[3]

Wilbur is generally a very friendly, sweet-natured dog (as are many dachshunds), but he certainly can become aggressive at the drop of a hat. If he catches a glimpse of someone walking or riding a bike down our road, he will shoot off the couch like a missile and bark ferociously! He'll stand with his front paws on the windowsill, growling and daring anybody to cross his territory. And heaven forbid when a delivery driver rings the doorbell ... He goes ballistic (as I'm sure most dogs do)!

Aside from the vacuum cleaner, Wilbur seems to have no fear of anyone or anything. Thankfully, he usually warms up to strangers quickly when I assure him there's no threat, and he has never bitten anyone. But I'm amazed by how bold and self-confident he can be,

---

[3] Source: www.ourdogs.co.uk/News/2008/July2008/News110708/dda.htm

especially considering his size. He must be unaware of how small he is since he's not even a little intimidated by a dog that's five times his size!

My dachshunds from childhood, Bridgett and Abby, were the exact same way when it came to other dogs or animals. Our house was quite far from the road, so we would let them out to do their business and roam freely several times a day. There was a Doberman pinscher in the neighborhood that belonged to a man who lived through the woods from us, and occasionally it would roam nearby. So when my dogs were outside, I was always nervous because of the Doberman. I never saw him come closer than fifty yards to our property, but if my dogs spotted him, they would take off running toward him down the field at full throttle, barking ferociously! Thankfully, this dog never once reciprocated my dogs' challenging behavior and would disappear nonchalantly in the woods before my dogs ever made it to him (although he had to have been terrified, *haha*!). Nevertheless, I was always very scared for my dogs because I knew that the Doberman could probably take them out with just one bite if he wanted to.

The dachshund's boldness and fearlessness have always intrigued me. It's so funny that these little dogs who stand only inches from the ground will charge monstrous-sized dogs without a moment's hesitation! Dachshunds are definitely full of themselves. Their bravery and fierce determination make me think of the story of David and Goliath: David looked up at this giant-of-a-man towering over him and declared battle with full confidence. He even refused to wear armor and told Goliath, "You come against me with sword and spear and javelin, but I come against you in the name of the Lord Almighty" (1 Samuel 17:45). As Goliath advanced toward David to attack him, David actually ran closer to him and gave Goliath a fatal blow to the head by slinging a stone at him (1 Samuel 17:48-49).

I can't help comparing the way David must have looked when charging at Goliath with the way my dachshunds looked as they took off through the field after that Doberman! It's comical, isn't it? But as you see in the story, David's confidence didn't come from trusting in himself or his own abilities—it came from his faith in an awesome, all-powerful God. And God certainly didn't let David down. I believe Christians need to realize that if we're up against a huge, overwhelming obstacle, it's okay to look silly and approach the battle like a dachshund charging at a Doberman ... as long as we're depending on God to deliver us and not on our own strength and devices.

Ready, Set, Charge!

There's a story about a battle in 2 Chronicles that captures the heart of the message I want you to grasp:

> Listen, King Jehoshaphat and all who live in Judah and Jerusalem! This is what the Lord says to you: *"Do not be afraid or discouraged because of this vast army. For the battle is not yours, but God's.* Tomorrow march down against them. They will be climbing up by the Pass of Ziz, and you will find them at the end of the gorge in the Desert of Jeruel. You will not have to fight this battle. Take up your positions; *stand firm and see the deliverance the Lord will give you*, Judah and Jerusalem. Do not be afraid; do not be discouraged. Go out to face them tomorrow, and the Lord will be with you" (2 Chronicles 20:15-17, emphasis mine).

As you can imagine, God showed up in this story. Despite being the underdogs, King Jehoshaphat and his men were soon celebrating a huge victory. Stories like this make me wonder how many times we've underestimated the strength and capabilities we have through God. All too often, I believe we give up our battles so easily because we only consider what we, ourselves, are able to do. We often forget Who we have on our team.

I believe it's about time for us to start putting some action behind the faith we claim to possess. I feel like God wants us to be more like a dachshund in some ways ... He wants us to fearlessly *act* upon the popular Scripture of Philippians 4:13, which states, "I can do all things through Christ who strengthens me" (NKJV). God wants us to charge toward our opponents with confidence and prove that we truly believe "we are more than conquerors through Him who loved us" (Romans 8:37, NKJV).

There's no doubt that we all have some pretty big mountains to climb in this fallen world we live in. But as Christians, we must never forget that we have a God on our side that's *way* bigger than any and every obstacle we face! Unless it's not within His sovereign will, we can overcome anything with God—absolutely nothing is impossible (Matthew 19:26). So, knowing that our Master has our backs, why not take on our giants with the fearlessness and confidence of the dachshund?!?

CHAPTER 12: KIBBLES AND BITS

Some things are hard to put nicely, so I'll just go ahead and say it—sometimes dogs really stink! All of them can give off some pretty foul odors. Of course, just like humans, dogs begin to smell bad if they go too long without a bath. Likewise, their breath can be quite offensive, especially if they eat something gross ... and that can lead to other smelly problems! Wilbur definitely has the stereotypical scent of a hound dog, and for some reason—despite the fact that I brush his teeth three times each week—his breath is worse than that of any other dog I've ever had.

Do you want to know something though? I actually like the way Wilbur smells! I know this probably sounds weird, but I love my Wilbur, and his "signature scent" is just a part of who he is ... I think I would like almost any scent that was *him*. This concept is nothing new under the sun; we all know that we can easily look (or sniff) past the flaws of those we love. Their "quirks" can even become attractive. Often when people talk about their significant other, they will say things like, "I love the fact that he/she is quirky." I believe it's just human nature to be drawn to individuals who stand out with unique characteristics because, if for no other reason, they are amusing or entertaining. Since we were made in God's image, I believe He loves uniqueness, too; by observing the vast variety in His creation, it's obvious that He does.

So my point is this: God loves some of the things about us that we or others may dislike. For His own reasons, God chose to give some people large noses, unusually wide hips, balding heads, and high-pitched, squeaky voices. He obviously wanted to make some people more attractive than others; some, more talented than others; and some, more intelligent than others. You get the point! While we all agree that there are certain qualities and features in people that the population at large considers to be unattractive, it doesn't work that way with God.

Most people have complaints about themselves—most often regarding traits they were born with. For example, I don't like being so short, but there's nothing I can do to change that. Obviously God likes me being 5'2" (or else He would've created me differently); still, I'm often guilty of wishing to be taller. Romans 9:20 has really convicted me of my negative self-appraisals, however. The verse asks:

> But who are you, a human being, to talk back to God?
> "Shall what is formed say to the one who formed it,
> 'Why did you make me like this?'"

Romans 9:21 continues with an analogy of a potter and his clay, emphasizing that God (the potter) has the right to make us (the clay) into whatever He chooses. This is a very strong argument against our negative self-judgment, isn't it? Why do we think we have a right to question or complain about our Creator's artwork when we are His masterpieces?

Our society puts forth many expectations, and it's hard not to compare ourselves to others as we strive to meet those expectations. However, as Christians, we should respect and appreciate God's craftsmanship. The feature that you like the least about yourself could be the one that God treasures the most because it's what makes you *you*. Perhaps it gives you the ability to fulfill the purpose(s) He created you for.

Most of us could certainly have more confidence in God's handiwork. I'll be the first to tell you that I need to practice what I've just preached *a lot* more ... and my husband and close loved ones would concur! Even still, I believe God loves us just the way we are. After all, He made us this way. So try not to judge your appearance or worth based on the standards of society. Be confident in your "signature scent," knowing that your Master cherishes it! I believe God intends for us to look at ourselves the way David thought of himself when he wrote:

> I praise you because I am fearfully and wonderfully made; your works are wonderful, I know that full well (Psalm 139:14).

Yuck!

Although I typically prefer Wilbur "au natural" versus smelling like his blueberry shampoo, I have a real change of heart when I see him do something gross. I've caught Wilbur doing some nasty things ... wallowing on decomposing animals, rummaging through smelly garbage, and eating unmentionable things! Even though I know these behaviors are typical of dogs, I'm so repulsed by them that sometimes I vow to never let Wilbur kiss me again! (Of course, I reconsider as soon as he's been cleaned up.) I'm sure if you're a dog owner, you can relate. Perhaps, like me, you've found yourself asking, *How on earth can a creature actually get pleasure from doing such gross things?!?*

One day when I was disgusted by something Wilbur had done, God revealed to me another parallel between my relationship with Wilbur and my relationship with Him. I believe He showed me that there's a strong resemblance between how I view Wilbur's nasty habits and the way He looks upon sin. God, being completely holy, probably can't even fathom how any sin could be enjoyable for us. However, this is where the concept of the Trinity (the Father, the Son, and the Holy Spirit) is extremely important to grasp because Jesus shared in our humanity and understands our desires. Although He didn't sin, He was tempted just as we are. Therefore, Jesus *understands* our fleshly nature ... But at the same time, I imagine God is repulsed by our sinful ways—much like we are disgusted by some of the things we see dogs do.

Thankfully, just as Wilbur's nasty habits do not keep me from loving him, God's feelings toward sin do not hinder His love for us. He proved that His love is unconditional by taking our filth upon Himself and dying on the cross in order to bridge the gap between the Holy and the unholy. Out of love, Jesus became the official "translator" between us and God; since He knows us *and* God intimately, He is "bilingual" and can bring understanding, love, and reconciliation between us. Thank the Lord we have a Master and Mediator who can bring God's healing and wholeness to our sin-sick souls when we can't speak the language of holiness. If we've been washed in the Blood of the Lamb, God dismisses our "grossness" and not only forgives us, but looks at us as if we are as clean and white as the freshly fallen snow (Isaiah 1:18). What a wonderful God!

<hr />

Forgiveness

Sin and forgiveness go hand in hand, so now I'm going to talk about one of the qualities I truly admire about Wilbur (as opposed to his nasty habits) ... his quickness to "forgive." Any time I've accidently stepped on his paw or hurt him in any way, Wilbur has accepted my apologies immediately. His tail wags and he kisses me, as if saying, *"It's okay, it's okay!!! I know you didn't mean to!"* Similarly, when I have scolded him, he's quick to recover. He may pout for a moment, but he's soon back to his sweet, loving self. In these situations, Wilbur seems to want to make amends quickly. He lowers his head and looks up at me with those precious, puppy-dog eyes, as if he's saying that he's sorry. It just melts my heart!

What I see in Wilbur is unconditional love and humility. He is so forgiving, and he lacks the pride to nurse a hurt. His humility often reminds me of what it truly means to forgive and love unconditionally. Dogs may not understand or know enough to have the challenges with forgiveness that we humans often face, but I think they set great examples of how God wants us to forgive and love others.

It's extremely difficult for us to lay our pride aside and extend forgiveness when we've been hurt. We usually want to make people pay when they have done us wrong rather than look at them through the eyes of Christ and extend grace and forgiveness. Our human nature likes to hold onto anger, bitterness, and resentment, doesn't it? As Christians, though, we are called to take a different path; we're supposed to renounce our prideful, begrudging natures. God doesn't want us to be doormats, but He does expect us to share the gifts of forgiveness and unconditional love which He has so freely given us.

I believe many people pray the Lord's Prayer without considering the implications of praying, "forgive us our sins, as we have forgiven those who sin against us." When Jesus finished teaching His disciples how to pray, He said this:

> For if you forgive other people when they sin against you, your heavenly Father will also forgive you. But if you do not forgive others their sins, your Father will not forgive your sins (Matthew 6:14-15).

Whew! That's definitely incentive to forgive, isn't it? Who among us can afford not to have their sins forgiven?

When we've been wronged, I think it's important for us to remember and believe that God is fair and that He promises to be our avenger. Hebrews 10:30 says, "For we know him who said, 'It is mine to avenge;

I will repay,' and again, 'The Lord will judge his people.'" So rather than playing judge, Paul tells us our job is this:

> Get rid of all bitterness, rage and anger, brawling and slander, along with every form of malice. Be kind and compassionate to one another, forgiving each other, just as in Christ God forgave you (Ephesians 4:31-32).

Basically, I think we need to take yet another lesson from our dogs! They are the ultimate forgivers. Unfortunately, everyone in our lives will likely let us down at times, and we will probably let them down as well. Rather than being known as people who hold grudges, we should be considered the peacemakers ... those who want to make amends quickly when conflicts occur. Harboring bitterness does nothing but destroy the body and soul. So even though we may not feel like it, we should extend forgiveness and unconditional love to others the way Christ has done for us. This will be extremely difficult sometimes, no doubt. But if dogs can do it, with the help of God, so can we!

CHAPTER 13: CARRIED AWAY

One of the countless things I love about Wilbur is the way he leaps into my arms when I bend down to pick him up. He doesn't just stand there and make me do all the work, he jumps full force! One day I thought about how much trust it would require for me to leap into the arms of a being that's about 10 times my height, not knowing where I was going. Just thinking about this made me realize how much faith Wilbur has in me.

I have also noticed that, aside from the times he obsesses over hiding a bone, Wilbur never seems to worry. I know that sounds silly, but think about it: Our pets don't seem to fret about where their next meal is coming from—at least Wilbur doesn't, anyway. Sometimes he may get hungry before we feed him and "tell" us that he wants or needs to eat, but I don't think he's ever doubted our ability to sustain him.

Sadly, I often fail to demonstrate this kind of faith in my Master. I'm usually reluctant to jump into God's arms when He wants to carry me to an unknown place, and I'm certainly guilty of worrying about my future at times. Jesus tells us if the birds of the air do not worry about where their next meal is coming from, we surely shouldn't, because we are far more valuable than they (Matthew 6:26). Yet we still worry, don't we?

I used to worry a lot. Everyone in my family told me that I could "worry the horns off a billy goat!" Thankfully, as I have matured in Christ, I've started to break my bad habit of worrying. My all-time favorite Scripture regarding worry, which has helped me more than anything, is Philippians 4:6-7. It says:

> Do not be anxious about anything, but in every situation, by prayer and petition, with thanksgiving, present your requests to God. And the peace of God, which transcends all understanding, will guard your hearts and your minds in Christ Jesus.

When I find myself beginning to fret over something, I recall these reassuring words and often repeat them to myself multiple times, allowing them to really sink in. I then pray about what's worrying me and give thanks to God in advance for what He's going to do to resolve the situation. Then, just as the Scripture promises, the supernatural peace of God comes over me and "guards" my heart and mind, giving me a feeling of calm assurance amidst the storm. I highly recommend memorizing this Scripture if you have a tendency to worry; it's sustained my sanity many times during troubling circumstances.

Our dogs may have an unfair advantage when it comes to worry since they don't really know enough to fear negative outcomes; however, I believe the faith they have in us is a prime example of how we should have complete faith in God to be our reliable provider. Worry does nothing but eat away at our mental, emotional, and physical health; and, ultimately, it represents a lack of faith in God and His sovereign will. The Master of all masters certainly deserves to have children who trust Him enough to turn their worries over to Him and jump full force into His mighty arms.

No Surprises!

One day I was sitting on the couch at home, awaiting the arrival of a home appraiser from the bank. We were seeking to refinance our house, and though this was a technicality, I had the house looking pretty spiffy and was anxious to finish this step in the process.

Wilbur, as usual, was just lying on my lap relaxing as I typed away on my computer. However, as soon as the appraiser's white car pulled up in our drive, Wilbur jumped up and started barking like crazy! He ran to the front window and jumped up, placing his front paws on the windowsill to get a better look outside. As he watched the man get out of the car and start up toward our house, Wilbur became even more ferocious and looked at me as if to say, *"Alert! Alert! Get ready for defense!"*

Every now and then, I appreciate Wilbur's "warnings," but this particular time I was just annoyed by him causing a big to-do over nothing. After all, I had been expecting this visitor all day. I tried to calm Wilbur down and assure him that everything was just fine, but as expected, this did no good. He was completely carried away, relentlessly trying to convince me that there was something to get worked up about. So I ended up having to put him behind closed doors.

After reflecting upon Wilbur's reaction to this harmless situation, I realized that I have acted like him in this respect at times. I've often tried to get God's attention and alert Him about something happening in my life when He's been expecting it all along.

God says: "I am the Alpha and the Omega, *the* Beginning and *the* End" (Revelation 1:8, NKJV). In other words, to Him, the future is as clear as the past. Psalm 139:4 tells us that God knows every single word that will ever come from our mouths, and verse 16 of that same Psalm tells us this:

> Your eyes saw my unformed body; all the days ordained
> for me were written in your book before one of them
> came to be.

Is that not fascinating? Everything you and I will ever say or do and everything that will ever happen in our lives was recorded in God's book long before He ever breathed life into us ... Not because we are programmed like robots, but because God has incredible foresight and knows exactly what choices and actions we will make as the result of our free will. Yet again, this boils down to the fact that God's knowledge and ways are unfathomably higher than our own. I find it very reassuring to know that my Master is anticipating everything that will ever happen in my life and that He knows how to help me get through every situation I will ever face.

There's an image and feeling I want you to capture as a result of reading this chapter and a specific Bible verse from Psalm 139 ... verse 5 says:

> You hem me in behind and before, and you lay your
> hand upon me.

When I first read this verse, I didn't get much out of it. Psalm 139 is one of my favorites, yet I just breezed over verse 5 every time I read it, not paying much attention to the words. But one day, I stopped and focused on this verse, trying to figure out what it meant to be "hemmed in" by God. Several images came to my mind. I envisioned myself as a little girl being tucked tightly into bed by my mom as she said, "Snug as a bug in a rug!" I also thought of a cocoon that completely envelops and protects the developing butterfly inside of it. Taking the verse literally, I pictured myself being sewn snugly between two soft pieces of fabric.

What kind of feeling do you get when you think of being "hemmed in" by God? I'm guessing, like me, you feel a sense of security. The vision of being nestled in, with God behind us and in front of us, should make us feel protected and safe. I believe this verse was intended to give us an illustration of God's closeness and also of His sovereignty over our pasts and futures.

Jesus assures us that we will have trouble in this life (John 16:33), but if God is our Father, we should never feel insecure again. The next time something alarms you and you're on the verge of getting carried away like Wilbur, remember that God already knows everything about your situation and is fully capable of handling it. He completely surrounds you like a cocoon and preserves you from the damage that the enemy tries to inflict upon you—whether it's related to your past or your future. Being present in all space and time, God already sees you triumphing over all the fears and trials in your lifetime (through Him) and is watching you fly through Heaven like a beautiful butterfly. So take a deep breath and relax. Trust God ... He's got you covered!

You're Going *This* Way!

As I write this, I have just returned home after taking Wilbur for a walk, though it might be more accurate to say that he took me on one! He always pulls me in the direction he wants to go, and most of the time I give in. For one reason, I know he needs to have the freedom to roam and follow the desires of his heart and nose from time to time. The other reason is that I don't feel like battling him. Believe me, he's so much stronger than he looks!

Without a doubt, Wilbur's favorite place to visit is the yard of my uncle and aunt, right up the street from our house. I'm pretty sure this is because they have a dog, a cat, goats, and some chickens! The smells coming from their yard are simply irresistible to Wilbur, and he just *has* to roam and sniff around there every time we walk. I jokingly refer to this yard as Wilbur's amusement park! Like a child who wants to prolong a fun day by riding just one more ride, Wilbur always resists leaving that much-loved place.

As a result, it's rather difficult for me to pull him away when I'm ready to continue walking. Not only is Wilbur strong, he's extremely stubborn! He weighs only 17 pounds, but he feels much heavier when he's determined to stay in one place. Even when I get frustrated with Wilbur's noncompliance, I can't pull him too hard because I'm scared one of us might get hurt (he has a sensitive back, and I have problematic shoulders). So when Wilbur refuses to budge, I have to pick him up and carry him. I often wonder what passersby think when they see a woman carrying a dachshund (wearing a harness and leash) down the street!

After one such struggle with Wilbur, I knelt down to pick him up and felt more frustrated than usual. I blurted out, "Wilbur, for crying out loud!!! What's the point?!? You're going this way whether you like it or not!" I continued thinking along these lines, *You know if you don't cooperate with me, I'm just going to carry you where I want to go!* Then, immediately I thought, *Hmmm … I bet this is exactly what God does with me sometimes.* There have been times when I've fought against God's leading, and He has had to show me the hard way that He's the boss!

God certainly doesn't force anyone to believe in or follow Him. However, if we have committed our lives to Jesus and He sees us wandering from His path, I believe He allows the consequences of our sins to break our will and teach us valuable lessons. If one of God's "lambs" continues to stray, I believe The Good Shepherd will allow something uncomfortable to happen to him so that he will draw close to his Shepherd. To relate this concept back to the original analogy, I believe God sometimes stoops down and carries us to a certain place, just as I do with Wilbur. He intervenes in our lives and redirects us toward the right path. Psalm 23:2-3 states:

> He *makes* me to lie down in green pastures;
> He leads me beside the still waters.
> He restores my soul;
> He leads me in the paths of righteousness
> For His name's sake (NKJV, emphasis mine).

It's significant that Scripture indicates there are times when God *makes* us lie down. I know there have been a few times in my life when

I was so preoccupied with worldly things that it took something significant, such as a health problem, to refocus my attention on God and His plans. During times of vulnerability, we tend to draw closer to God, "our refuge and strength, a very present help in trouble" (Psalm 46:1, NKJV). So, can you think of a time when God has figuratively reached down, lifted you up, and carried you to a place you didn't want to go in order to regain your attention and focus? Was it perhaps due to rebellion against God or His ways? I'm sure, like myself, many of you can look back and see some times when God completely took over the reins in your life. One verse in the Bible that comes to mind regarding this topic is Proverbs 16:9, which states:

> We can make our plans, but the Lord determines our
> steps (NLT).

We can be "Type A" people and map out every little detail of our lives, but if our plans don't align with God's will, He can intervene and totally change our courses. The goal of every Christian should be for his or her will to match up with the will of God—this means we should strive to be obedient to Him and follow His leading. In doing so, we will voluntarily go down more of the right paths, and our lives will go much more smoothly. However, when we find ourselves in Wilbur's position, being taken in the opposite direction of where we want to go, we might as well give up the fight of resistance … We should just sink into our Master's arms and make the most of the ride.

Life is full of worries and surprises, but here's the run-down of some helpful advice I can give based on my experiences with Wilbur: Don't get carried away; instead, allow God to carry you. Jump full force into His arms and be confident in His ability to get you through every storm. If He decides to take you somewhere against your will, have faith that His "detour" is necessary. Remember that, ultimately, the place God wants to carry you is closer to Him. So if you trust and follow the Master (the Good Shepherd), sooner or later you'll find yourself roaming in greener pastures!

CHAPTER 14: HEART'S DESIRE

Lately I've been a little concerned about Wilbur's mental health … seriously! He's been rather withdrawn, moping around with a pouty expression more often than I think is normal. My cousin recently saw Wilbur and evidently thought he looked sad, too, because she looked at him with concern and asked, "What's wrong, Wilbur?"

I know it's quite common for dogs to pout every now and then, but unfortunately, I'm starting to think Wilbur may be a little depressed. Thankfully, it's easy to perk him up; his sad eyes quickly come to life when I throw his squeaky toy, tell him we're going for a walk, or allow him to chase after his little mobile hamster. So it's likely that Wilbur's real problem is plain old boredom. Since dachshunds were bred to hunt, it makes sense that Wilbur gets down when he has nothing to do but lie around. Sometimes I think he would be happier with a fellow doggie companion, but I'm not sure that's the answer.

The dachshunds I've had in the past seemed content to sleep most of the time, but Wilbur requires more stimulation and activity. I often feel guilty for confining him to life as a house dog, knowing that he'd probably be happier if he could roam freely outside. Some of our neighbors have had dachshunds that were allowed to come and go as they pleased, and they seemed so happy, snooping around here, there, and everywhere. Unfortunately, many of them met untimely ends in the road. I doubt Wilbur would make it a day before suffering the same fate, so letting him have free range just isn't an option.

Unfortunately, I see a reflection of my former self in Wilbur when he mopes around, seemingly bored and dissatisfied. For much of my life, I was unfulfilled, too. You see, I've always had a deep-rooted desire to fulfill God's specific purposes in my life, but for a long time I didn't feel like I was on the right path. I didn't know exactly what God was calling me to do with my life, but for many years I knew that nursing was not my *true* calling.

Although I graduated third in my high school class, academics and a career were never my real goals. To be honest, I would've been perfectly happy getting married and starting a family straight out of high school, though for various reasons, that was not to be. So I knew I needed to go to college and that I should probably do something in the medical field. My mom is a nurse, and I had always admired her for being able to give medical advice, check blood pressure, remove sutures, and help people in similar ways. Her anatomy and nursing books also fascinated me. So when I found out I could get a full college scholarship to become a nurse if I agreed to work in North Carolina for four years after graduation, I decided to pursue nursing.

Within just a few weeks of starting nursing school, however, I began to have doubts about my career choice; I feared that I wouldn't find complete fulfillment working as a nurse. I tried to be optimistic, thinking I could always go back to graduate school to become a nurse practitioner or a nurse anesthetist, but I was still discouraged. Regardless of what I might do, I knew I couldn't afford to back out of the plan. If I did, I would have to pay back all my scholarship money, plus interest. So, ultimately, financial concerns were the incentive that got me through nursing school and those first four years of nursing.

I find it hard to believe that it's now been more than 12 years since I graduated from college. I've had many different nursing positions in a variety of settings since then. Throughout my career, I've had many rewarding experiences, especially over the last few years of working with hospice patients and their families. They often call me an angel and tell me what a meaningful difference I've made in their lives during a difficult time. I feel great satisfaction in knowing that God has used me as an instrument to provide tender loving care to many people. Still, more often than not, I've been unsettled and discontent in my nursing career.

Something inside me kept searching for something more, and there was an empty spot in my heart that seemed to be getting deeper and deeper. I didn't know what I wanted to do, except that I wished I could help people on a deeper emotional and spiritual level. As a nurse, it's often a huge challenge just to meet the physical needs of my patients and to complete the necessary charting, so it's next to impossible to find the time to interact with people the way I'd like to. I considered the possibility of becoming a spiritual counselor, chaplain, or missionary—anything that would allow me to better incorporate my Christian faith into my professional life. Still, I had no clear direction that warranted a career change.

Although I enjoyed working with my wonderful coworkers and took pride in being a competent and compassionate nurse, my dissatisfaction began to take its toll. I stayed stressed out, physically and emotionally, and I often felt spiritually unfulfilled. My work as a nurse was all-consuming, and because my heart wasn't fully in it, I began to feel burned-out and wasted ... There didn't seem to be much of the *real me* left.

Sweet Freedom

Thankfully, after many prayers and a lot of searching, I began to see the direction God was leading me—my calling finally began to come into focus. About five years ago, I sensed that God wanted me to start taking notes of the various insights that He planted in my mind (which revolved around analogies between the natural and spiritual realms). So

I began to write down anything and everything I felt God was "telling" me. Many times I remember scribbling down ideas that crossed my mind on a scrap sheet of paper while at work or even in line at the grocery store. I would stash all my notes in the nightstand drawer beside my bed, and I sensed that I was eventually going to write a book from the material I was accumulating. About three years ago, I got the feeling that it was time—time to start writing a book.

I have enjoyed writing for as long as I can remember. I started writing poems when I was about 11 years old, and I found that I could express myself and my feelings much better on paper than in person. So it wasn't a huge surprise to me when I sensed that God was calling me to write a book. I remember sitting down on the couch with my laptop and all of my unorganized sheets of paper one day in December of 2010, and I just started typing away. I felt such peace and satisfaction when I wrote; I was in my element, so to speak. The more I wrote, the more I desired to write, and the more God gave me to write about. So I became convinced that my God-given calling was to evangelize and minister to others through writing, and that calling was confirmed time and time again.

With the support of my husband, I gradually made some changes in my work schedule, changes which allowed me more time to dedicate to writing. Thanks to God and my husband, I now work as a nurse only a few days each month and spend the rest of my time writing and being a better wife and housekeeper. My life is drastically different than it was several years ago, and I'm experiencing contentment and peace like never before. Although I don't want to completely give up nursing (since I find much meaning and satisfaction in providing hospice care), I'm thankful that it is no longer my primary focus. I'm no longer weighed down by that heavy, empty feeling that consumed me. My wandering spirit is now replaced by what I can best describe as a deep sense of knowing ... knowing that I'm finally on the right path toward accomplishing my life's purpose.

That's not to say that my life is now worry-free. I still have problems, stresses, and concerns—don't we all! My husband and I have had to make some financial sacrifices in order to fulfill God's call, and we've had our share of adversity. Since I have made changes in my career, we have encountered a few not-so-subtle remarks of disapproval. It just isn't normal for a childless woman with a solid career to stay home in our fast-paced, materialistic society. I feel that I am no longer living up to the expectations that family and society had for me, and there have been plenty of times when I've wished that my primary calling was to be a nurse. It would be so much simpler to continue doing a noble, respected job that I already know how to do instead of "going against the grain" and pursuing a writing career. When I tell people that I am now primarily focused on writing a book (with my dog's name on the title, at that!) rather than working as a nurse, I believe most of them secretly think I'm crazy. To be honest, the judgmental attitudes hurt my feelings more than I'd like to admit.

Thankfully, my husband and I are mature enough in our faith and in our marriage not to allow the opinions of others to dissuade us from our new lifestyle. We know that we're being obedient to God and that He is now my official "boss." I may not make much money as a writer, but I'm working for the highest-paying Man around, and His rewards are the only ones I can take with me when I leave this earth.

It's a wonderful blessing to finally be free to be me instead of the *me* everyone expects. Do I know where this road is leading? No, I don't. God does, however, and I trust that He will provide. I'm clinging to the promise God makes in Psalm 37:4:

> Take delight in the Lord, and he will give you the desires of your heart.

What about you? Are you living the life God intends for you? Do you even have a clue of what that life looks like? If not, I suggest you be in prayer and fellowship with God until you feel His promptings; He'll lead you in the direction He wants you to go. If you already know what He is calling you to do and feel that you aren't being true to that calling, what are you waiting for? Believe me, if God is calling you to do something different with your life, you can't tune out His voice. Now is the time to act!

Perhaps you feel trapped in a life you weren't intended to live, just as I did. You may feel like a captive, longing to escape your bonds. This could be boredom, like Wilbur feels when he can't go out to play, or this could be the Holy Spirit letting you know that He wants more for you. It may take much prayer, time, and patience to receive clear guidance from God, but once you're sure of your mission, I encourage you to pursue it with all your might. I know from experience that it's difficult to be truly content doing anything else.

Each of us, including you, is a unique and valuable work of art created by God. Ephesians 2:10 tells us that "we are God's handiwork, created in Christ Jesus to do good works, which God prepared in advance for us to do." Just as each individual body part is important and necessary for the body as a whole to be fully functional, every believer and his or her contributions are crucial to the overall well-being of the body of Christ (see 1 Corinthians 12). There is certainly not a shortage of needs in this dark and hurting world; so, whether God has called you to be a missionary, cook, janitor, teacher, doctor, entrepreneur, or stay-at-home mother, you need to believe that your job is important and necessary and do it for the glory of God.

Colossians 3:23-24 says:

> Whatever you do, work at it with all your heart, as working for the Lord, not for human masters, since you know that you will receive an inheritance from the Lord as a reward. It is the Lord Christ you are serving.

If you abide by this Scripture and do the work God is calling you to do, you will have joy and fulfillment. Will it be difficult at times? Certainly. Will you feel stressed when challenges arise? Most likely, yes. Will you get rich in the financial sense? Maybe, but probably not. Will your reward be great and lasting? Absolutely! There's great satisfaction in everything you do when your master is the Lord and you are working for His glory.

Unlike Wilbur, I was able to make changes in my life that eased my discontent. Wilbur can't change his circumstances, and there is little I can do to ease the apparent boredom he experiences at times. I try to take him outside more often, but I can't turn him loose to trail rabbits … I can't encourage him to pursue his passion to be the hunter he was born to be. However, I can encourage you. If God is calling you in a different direction, I hope my story helps you take the first step. This life is way too short for you to settle for being anyone other than the *you* God created you to be!

CHAPTER 15: LOYALTY LIKE NONE OTHER

L oyalty is a trait dogs are known for, and I believe this is why they are considered to be man's best friend. For the most part, dogs are loving companions who offer us unconditional love. If you gain 50 pounds and grow old and wrinkly, so what? A dog's love and affection will be unchanged. It makes no difference if we are rich or poor; gorgeous or not; a worldwide celebrity or an average Joe, a dog will always offer a warm welcome at the door with a wagging tail and kisses—regardless of our mood at the time.

It's wonderful to experience that kind of unconditional love and loyalty from another living creature. Let's face it—human love is quite different. Circumstances significantly influence how even our closest family members treat us and how we treat them. So it's nice to be able to count on Wilbur's affection when I'm in a bad mood and to know that he will still enjoy kissing me when I've been sick and in bed all day—even if I haven't brushed my teeth or showered!

Wilbur certainly likes to chase things, chew bones, and get into trouble; but I believe his two top priorities in life are to be loved by my husband and me and to love (and protect) us in return. Wilbur loves my husband, but he's usually a Momma's boy. If given the choice,

99 percent of the time he will sit in my lap while we relax in the living room. His partiality and loyalty toward me really warm my heart!

Recently, just for fun, I decided to put Wilbur's loyalty and protective instincts over me to the test. My husband sometimes plays a game by shaping his hand to resemble the mouth of an alligator and coming slowly toward Wilbur in a "chomping" motion to aggravate him and get him riled up. Wilbur, perhaps associating this action with having his bone taken away or having his ears messed with (which he hates), gets pretty fired up when my husband does this. He typically growls, barks, and nips at my husband's hand. So, wanting to test Wilbur out, I told my husband to threaten *me* with the "alligator hand." Wow!!! When he did this, we were both astounded to see how aggressive Wilbur became in defending me. He instantly changed from a sweet, humble little dog to a snarling, striking beast! He curled up his lip, exposed his teeth, and growled like the demons in *The Exorcist*, and then he lunged at my husband's hand in a serious attempt to bite it.

My husband and I couldn't believe Wilbur's radical transformation because he had never acted that way or attempted to bite before, but I have to admit that Wilbur's reaction really impressed me. I was touched to see that he loved me so much—to know that he was that loyal to and protective of me. After our little "game" ended, I nuzzled and kissed my Wilbur and praised him for being such a courageous defender! I doubt I'll ever forget how Wilbur proved his loyalty to me that evening.

A dog's genuine dedication to his master is certainly an admirable quality. My husband and I recently watched an excellent movie, *Hachi: A Dog's Tale*, based on a true story. This movie displays the perfect example of a dog's loyalty. Ladies, I highly recommend watching it after you have removed your makeup! Even though it's likely to stir up some tears, this movie is well worth watching to see the depth of love and devotion that the dog, Hachi, displayed toward his favorite human companion.

Hot or Cold?

I believe we humans need to learn a few things about loyalty from our dogs. I know there are some people who are exceptionally loving and loyal, but overall, I think we all have room for improvement. I can say for sure that I do. By the world's standards, I consider myself to be a loyal person. I have always wanted to be close to my loved ones and have lived within minutes of my mom, grandparents, and some aunts and uncles nearly all of my life (my house is on family land). I've had the same best friend since second grade, and as far as relationships go, I've never cheated on anyone. For these reasons, I believe most people would consider me a loyal person.

Regretfully, when it comes to my relationship with God, I have had my share of disloyalty. I have been disobedient to God many times, even after being convicted of my sins; I have turned my back on His will and chosen to go my own way, leaving Him in the back seat. I'm surely not proud of my disloyalty to God, and I've inevitably paid the price for it one way or another—as we all eventually do when we sin against Him.

I know I should be more like Wilbur when it comes to being loyal to my Master, keeping my focus on Him and sticking close by His side. I should be more devoted and diligent in seeking His Kingdom and His glory rather than being sidetracked by the distractions of my fleshly nature. The Bible says it plainly:

> No one can serve two masters. Either you will hate the one and love the other, or you will be devoted to the one and despise the other (Matthew 6:24).

To paraphrase this Scripture: It's impossible to be loyal to this world and its expectations AND be loyal to God and His standards at the same time.

People are often ridiculed for having strong morals and going against the norms of society. The values and lifestyles of mainstream Americans and devoted Christians are growing further and further apart, to the point where many people view Christians as intolerant bigots. In the eyes of many, pop culture and God just don't mix. But God makes it very clear that He doesn't want mediocre followers who try to walk on the "in- between" line, as I believe many people attempt to do today. He expects our whole hearts or else we may as well give Him nothing at all. In Revelation, Jesus says:

> I know your deeds, that you are neither cold nor hot. I wish you were either one or the other! So, because you are lukewarm—neither hot nor cold—I am about to spit you out of my mouth (3:15-16).

This is an eye-opening Scripture, and it calls us to evaluate our loyalty to God.

Who's #1?

A dog's loyalty develops as a result of getting to know and trust his master, and so it is between us and God. The more we know the Lord, the more we love Him; and the more we love Him, the more loyal to Him we become. If you don't truly know the Master, I think it's impossible to be genuinely loyal to Him. I believe this is why the Bible makes it clear that it isn't enough for a person to simply *believe* there is a God and that Jesus Christ came to save mankind from sin; even the devil "believes" in God (James 2:19), yet he is the poster child of disloyalty.

Now is a good time to discuss some topics and verses in Scripture that are very disturbing to me. To be honest, I find them downright scary. Nevertheless, I believe that "all Scripture is God-breathed and is useful for teaching, rebuking, correcting and training in righteousness" (2 Timothy 3:16). Out of love and concern for each person reading this book, I have an obligation to share and discuss Matthew 7:21-23, which states:

Not everyone who says to me, "Lord, Lord," will enter the kingdom of heaven, but only the one who does the will of my Father who is in heaven. *Many* will say to me on that day, "Lord, Lord, did we not prophesy in your name and in your name drive out demons and in your name perform many miracles?" Then I will tell them plainly, *"I never knew you. Away from me, you evildoers!"* (emphasis mine).

I'm guessing these verses are bothersome to you as well. It's hard enough for me to imagine a murderer enduring eternal separation from God in Hell, much less a person who has proclaimed to be Christian and served in Christ's name. It's extremely disturbing to me to think that there are many people who think they are "saved," yet they're not. Based on Matthew 7:21-23, I believe there are many people who *believe* in God and Jesus, but they don't really *know* Him or have a personal relationship with Him.

A person can attend church every time the doors are open for their entire life and still not be Heaven-bound. I've often heard the famous preacher and speaker, Joyce Meyer, say "Just because you go to church doesn't mean you're a Christian. I can go sit in the garage all day and it doesn't make me a car."[4] It really concerns me that there are many people in our society today who go to church, wear cross necklaces, and profess to be Christian, yet they live no differently than nonbelievers.

Of course, nobody is perfect or else we wouldn't need a Savior. But I believe people who are truly right with God have a personal relationship with Him, which consists of a general mindfulness of God and frequent communication with Him through prayer. Such people habitually seek God, desiring to know Him better and to be loyal to Him and His commandments. I believe they also long to give of themselves and

---

[4] Source: http://www.goodreads.com/author/quotes/8352.Joyce Meyer

their resources to help advance God's Kingdom. To sum it up, I believe genuine followers of Christ strive to love God with all their heart, soul, strength, and mind and to love their neighbors as themselves, as God commands in Luke 10:27.

If you are living outside the will of God, like many people in our society today, and you don't feel convicted or compelled to live a more God-honoring life, I beg you to consider your true standing with Him. God is a jealous God (Deuteronomy 4:24), and He commands us in the very first of the Ten Commandments to have no other gods before Him (Exodus 20:3). It isn't easy to keep God first when the cares of this world fight for our attention; it takes much effort to keep our relationship with Him top priority. But God expects nothing to take precedence over Him and His call on our lives—not our friends, not other people's opinions, not even our own families.

I believe many people in our society have made money their god, perhaps without truly realizing it. There is nothing sinful about prosperity; in fact, God promises to bless those who give Him the first 10 percent of their income with so much that they won't even be able to contain the blessings (Malachi 3:10). However, "the *love* of money is a root of all kinds of evil," and "some people, eager for money, have wandered from the faith and pierced themselves with many griefs" (1 Timothy 6:10, emphasis mine).

I think the most important question to consider is simple: Who or what do you *truly* love and value most in life? Is it God? Your family? Success? Yourself? The Bible says, "For where your treasure is, there your heart will be also" (Matthew 6:21). I consider your "treasure" to be that to which you devote most of yourself—the person or thing that consumes most of your thoughts, time, and resources. If God isn't your true treasure, I believe it's important for you to realize and acknowledge that you aren't being loyal to Him.

Hot Topic

The topic of our loyalty to God is an uncomfortable one because it forces us to evaluate our real priorities in light of our relationship with Him. I'm discussing these sensitive topics only because I have much love and compassion for people and can't stand the thought of anyone perishing. Unfortunately, I believe many churches today avoid the topic of Hell out of fear that it will scare people away. Many people, including some who consider themselves to be Christian, do not believe in a literal Hell because they feel that a loving God could not allow people to suffer eternally. I'd like to believe that there's no such place, but since I believe the Bible is God's absolute truth, I have no choice but to believe in a literal Hell.

The Bible actually mentions Hell more times than it does Heaven and states that *most* people will spend eternity in this terrible place. Jesus says that on the judgment day, He will reject many people who claimed to follow Him. This seems extreme, right? Yet in the same chapter, He also says:

> Enter through the narrow gate. For wide is the gate and broad is the road that leads to destruction, and *many* enter through it. But small is the gate and narrow the road that leads to life, and only *a few* find it (Matthew 7:13-14, emphasis mine).

I can't explain how or why so many people will perish, and I have many questions surrounding this subject. However, I know that God, who is completely holy and sinless; all-knowing and sovereign; and who sees inside the heart of every man, is fully entitled and qualified to judge His creation. After many deep conversations about Hell with Christian friends and family, I have concluded that it will remain a disturbing mystery to us all. But there are some concepts regarding this topic that I find easy to understand, so I'm going to share what I *do* know...

Scripture says, "For what do righteousness and wickedness have in common? Or what fellowship can light have with darkness?" (2 Corinthians 6:14). This verse tells us that evil and sin cannot coexist with God in His heavenly realm. Yet God loves us sinners so much and wants to have eternal fellowship with us so badly that He left the splendor and holiness of Heaven to become a man and live in this evil world. He walked among men and experienced temptation and pain just like we do, but He didn't sin. He remained a pure and spotless lamb—a perfect sacrifice—to take our sins upon Himself.

Since "the wages of sin is death" (Romans 6:23), Jesus had to give up His very life to fully pay off the debt of our sins. He stood in as our substitute and endured the punishment for all the evil that has ever existed or ever will exist in this terrible world. He suffered an unfathomable amount of physical and emotional pain and then died for the sins of you, me, and every human being who has ever lived (and all who ever will live). The key message of the Bible is that, despite our sin, God loves us so much that He has made a way to be with us forever. Everyone who acknowledges and confesses that they have sinned against Him and makes Jesus Christ their Lord and Savior will live eternally with Him in Heaven.

God has *offered* the gift of eternal life to every single person—serial killers, doctors, terrorists, teachers, rapists, and nuns alike. But here's the deal: He's not going to *open* the gift for anybody. Each and every person has a beautifully wrapped package right in front of him or her. For whatever reason, though, many people ignore or choose not to open the gift, and the outcome for these people is very unfortunate. However, they chose not to accept the gift, so it's important to remember that the choice and loss were *theirs*. Does it make sense to consider God unloving, unfair, and harsh if people willfully refuse the gift He offers? The gift He intended for their ultimate good? The answer is obviously no.

Consider another everyday life illustration of this concept: Is a cashier unjust to charge a person full price for an item because there was a coupon in the Sunday paper that the customer failed to redeem? Again, the answer is obviously no. Unfortunately, the full price of sin is death and Hell, which was originally created for Lucifer and his followers who rebelled against God in Heaven before the creation of the earth (see Matthew 25:41). God never intended for any *person* to go to Hell. So when Adam and Eve (who represented all of humankind) fell into the devil's snare and rebelled against Him, God implemented Plan B ... reconciliation between The Holy and the unholy through the atoning blood of His Son, Jesus Christ. Thankfully, Someone came to our rescue and was willing to pay the high price for our sins, giving us an escape pass from Hell.

The Word says God is patient, wanting all to come to Him in repentance so that no one will have to perish (2 Peter 3:9, paraphrased). But it's up to each of us individually to take advantage of the awesome *coupon* we've been given and to present it to God upon our *check out*—or else we will be responsible for paying the price of our sins in full. I cannot and do not want to imagine just how expensive the full price of sin is. Books and television shows have recounted stories of people who describe near-death experiences in Hell; there are no words to describe how I feel inside when I hear of such accounts and picture multitudes of souls enduring unimaginable torment forever and ever.

This topic really hits me hard, perhaps because I'm a hospice nurse and have watched many people take their last breaths and slip into eternity. I have experienced the supernatural and have witnessed vast differences between the deaths of believers and nonbelievers. God, Satan, Heaven, and Hell are real, folks. They are definitely no joke! The stakes are extremely high, so I hope and pray that you all accept God's precious gift of salvation before it's too late. It is beyond tragic for anybody to pass up the best gift ever given and end up in the worst place imaginable for eternity.

The Master's Order

In contrast to the consequences of failing to give one's loyalty to God, let's talk about what it means to be completely sold out to the Master. God has entrusted those of us who have a genuine relationship with Him with the most valuable gift on earth ... the Truth that has the power to change lives here and for eternity. Christians have the ability (through the power of the Holy Spirit) to shed Light into this dark world. And because we are abundantly blessed with the hope and reward of eternal life, God expects much from us (see Luke 12:48).

In Matthew 28:19-20, Jesus instructs His followers to go throughout the world, preaching and teaching His messages and commandments. This "Great Commission" to which He has called us is extremely important to our Master, so we should be devoted and dedicated to fulfilling it. We need not leave our towns, and likely not even our streets, to find someone who needs to hear the Truth.

There are likely many people around you (probably even some you are very close to) who are spiritually drowning, their eternal destinies in jeopardy. If you truly care about them and about fulfilling the purposes of God, you need to offer them the Life Preserver. If you passed a person who was drowning in a pond, would you simply glance at them and walk on by? I sure hope not—yet that's what you (and I) may be doing in the spiritual realm every day. Unfortunately, there are many "good" and "nice" people who don't have a relationship with Christ and are on the road to Hell this very moment. So instead of making the usual small talk about the football game last night or the weather, be courageous and ask your neighbor or your coworkers if they know Jesus.

I have often thought about the irony of my job as a hospice nurse. The whole purpose of hospice care is to keep people as comfortable and pain-free as possible as they leave this world. I've had several self-proclaimed "nonspiritual" patients that I have worked so hard for in their last hours in an attempt to keep them comfortable. Every time I turned around, I was giving them more medication (often drugs more potent than morphine), trying my best to manage their symptoms of pain, agitation, or shortness of breath. As I administered IV narcotics to some of these patients, I saw them stare up at the ceiling with tears and looks of sheer terror in their eyes as they moaned and jerked their bodies to the left and right (as if they were trying to dodge something). There have been a few times when I've had to fight back tears as I stood at the bedside feeling helpless with the "big gun" medications in hand; I knew that even if the medications helped alleviate these patients' symptoms, it would probably be for only a little while longer. With each minute that passed, I felt like these people were getting closer and closer to the point of no return—to a place where I (nor any doctor or medication) could do absolutely nothing to help them. The emotions I've experienced at times like these are impossible to describe in words.

The irony is that it's senseless to keep people comfortable in the here and now by avoiding topics that they would rather not discuss, such as God, faith, and their eternal destinies, yet do absolutely nothing to try to prevent them from being in pain and misery for eternity! In actuality, we should be doing just the opposite. Wouldn't you rather risk making someone you love upset or uncomfortable in order to decrease the odds of them being tormented forever?

God wants and expects His children to plant some good seeds into the lives of people and to keep those seeds watered; He doesn't ask or expect us to make flowers grow. That's His job. We can simply speak a few words about the Lord to someone, and then perhaps they will be more receptive to the calling of the Holy Spirit; "for the word of God is living and powerful, and sharper than any two-edged sword" (Hebrews 4:12, NKJV). Even just a simple statement like, "I'll be praying for you," may make a huge impact on someone. The power of the Holy Spirit is so strong that if we can ignite a small spark inside of someone's soul, he or she may catch fire for the Lord.

◦━━━━◦

I recently passed a billboard that captured my attention. The wording was brief and to the point: "Life is short. Eternity is not." Think about the implication of those two statements. We all know that life can end without a moment's notice, and whether one believes it or not, immediately after death there is eternity. If you don't know for sure that you will spend it with God, please take a moment right now to ask Jesus into your heart as your Savior and Lord, and then seek Christian counsel and fellowship.[5] If you're already a child of God and know people who aren't, please pray for them and talk with them as soon as possible.

The Gospel of Christ can be uncomfortable at times. People may get angry or offended when confronted with God's Word. However, I'm not ashamed for speaking the Truth (without "watering it down"), nor am I bothered that people may call me a radical religious fanatic. God has called me—just as He calls all of us—to share Jesus with others, no matter how deep and difficult the discussions may be. As the moral fabric in our nation continues to deteriorate and signs of Christ's return appear all around us, I'm more passionate than ever to share the Good News and to warn people of the eternal consequences involved with rejecting it.

I want to be loyal to my Master, just as Wilbur is loyal to me. I want to follow Him whole-heartedly and to fight for His cause by obeying His Great Commission. Writing this book is certainly my greatest attempt to be loyal to Him. I hope and pray to continue doing all I can

---

[5] If you have questions about how to have a relationship with Jesus Christ, call 1-800-JESUS-2000. Learn more about how you can experience the kind of life God intends for you. And if you don't have a church home, find a family of believers in your community who will support you in your spiritual growth.

to help build up Christ's Kingdom, and I hope I've convinced you to strive for this as well. Going "all in" for God involves some risks, no doubt. But, ultimately, we are guaranteed to win with Him by our sides. Remember that God went "all in" for us, demonstrating the perfect example of loyalty by laying down His life on our behalves. He's the most faithful friend and Master we can ever find, promising to never leave or forsake us (Hebrews 13:5); therefore, He is so deserving of our attempts to reciprocate this kind of devotion.

CHAPTER 16: LAUREN'S LEGACY

Before officially starting this chapter, you should know that the remaining chapters will be quite different from the preceding ones. There will not be any new analogies regarding Wilbur; however, I will be revisiting some themes and verses from previous analogies as they pertain to what I want to share.

My life was forever changed on July 16, 2013, at approximately 10:00 p.m., when I saw my husband, mom, and stepdad at the front door of my workplace. The moment I saw them there, I knew my life was never going to be the same. As they approached me and I saw the looks on their faces, I felt my heart drop. I anticipated and tried to prepare myself for the news that one of my grandparents, or perhaps even my dad, had died. As my mind churned with questions and my heart raced, my family pulled me into a secluded conference room and told me that my 11-year-old cousin and godchild, Lauren (affection-ately known as "Snuckums"), had just died. I'll never forget looking into my mom's tearful eyes and hearing her voice crack when she said the dreadful words, "Our baby's gone!"

Lauren was at swim team practice in a local community pool when a power line fell from a pole over 50 feet away. The live wire sent elec-trical current through the rain-soaked ground and into the pool, and the water was reported to feel "tingly." So everyone was instructed to get out of the pool, and when Lauren grabbed the metal ladder to do so, she was electrocuted. My cousin Lori, Lauren's mother, witnessed every horrific detail. Lifeguards, paramedics, nurses, and doctors performed CPR for an hour before surrendering, and then the terrible news was delivered to a large crowd of people gathered in the waiting area of the local emergency room. I'm glad I was at work that evening ... I can't imagine how thick the grief must have been in that hospital, and I'm thankful God spared me from that experience.

My initial response to this devastating news was complete shock; the entire story seemed too bizarre to be true. Somehow, I was able to finish charting the medications I had administered to my patients that evening, and my family then drove me home from work. Reality and despair hit quickly when I saw my 84-year-old grandfather crying and holding his chest, saying, "Dear Lord, why couldn't it have been me? I've lived my life and am ready to go!" I just sat in the chair with him and sobbed, sharing the grief that everyone in my family was experiencing.

That night was by far the worst night of our lives. One minute, things were going on as usual and the next, my family was gathered in my grandparents' living room discussing the organs that were being donated by "our" precious little girl—the only child in our close-knit family. I'm surprised at the physical pain that has accompanied the emotional turmoil. It feels like a knife stabs me in the chest each time a new wave of tears begins to flow.

At the time of Lauren's death, I was essentially finished with the rough draft of this book, but since this has been a life-changing event in my life and the lives of my loved ones, there was no way I could send it off to the press without including Lauren's story. I want to take advantage of the opportunity I have to honor Lauren by dedicating this book to her. I also want to honor her by sharing some things about her and about the spiritual insights I've gained as a result of reflecting upon her life and death.

Lauren = Love + Laughter

Lauren was a precious gift from God to so many people. Mere words can't paint a picture of her, but I believe Lauren can best be described as a bright, warm ray of sunshine who shined light, love, and joy on everything and everyone she touched. Lauren and I shared a kindred spirit in some ways, especially when it came to our love of dogs. Lauren always smiled extra wide and giggled extra loud when she was around dogs, and she took up with any and every dog that roamed our neighborhood. She was so excited when she received a puppy to call her own nearly five years ago. Lauren absolutely adored her Shih-poo, C.C., who she viewed as a cross between her baby and her sister.

Lauren was fond of Wilbur, too. In October 2012, I decided to enter a photo of Wilbur in a Halloween photo contest, so I enlisted Lauren to help. With my grandfather's generous help, I set up a traditional fall scene, complete with gourds, pumpkins, hay, and a Jack-O-Lantern that said "Happy Halloweenie!" I dressed Wilbur in a hotdog costume and staged Lauren and other family members around a campfire, roasting hotdogs and enjoying a nice fall evening. (Wilbur wasn't too happy about the costume, so I spent much of the evening trying to get him into place!) The photo I chose to enter into the competition shows Wilbur looking at a real hotdog and Lauren in the background, smiling as she sits by the fire. The next week, Lauren told me that she had written a story about our family's fall cookout and Wilbur's photo shoot. Even though we didn't win the contest, Lauren and I agreed that we had fun trying, and we laughed about the good memories we made.

Lauren loved her family. She didn't seem to mind being the only child in my extended family because she always recruited adult playmates. She absolutely loved to play and probably had the most vivid imagination of anyone I've ever known. She often had her grandparents marching around in circles, pretending to play instruments in the marching band, or sitting at their "desks," acting like students in her classroom. Lauren somehow even managed to get her great grand-mother (my "Granny") on her trampoline!

At our last family beach trip with Lauren, she pretended to be a tattoo artist and gave nearly everyone in the family at least one fake, glittery tattoo! (I actually liked sporting her pretty butterfly design on my back the whole week.) Lauren definitely enhanced our beach trips. She was very entertaining, going nonstop from the time she woke up until her bedtime—skipping back and forth between the beach, the pool, and the kitchen for snacks (she loved to eat!). It was a riot watch-ing Lauren play putt-putt, too. Everyone laughed as she guided the ball in the hole after about 30 strokes and then yelled out to her dad, the scorekeeper, "Daddy, I got a 2!"

Some of my all-time favorite memories of Lauren involve a puppet named "I-need-a" Nurse (also known as "Anita"). My mom bought the puppet years ago to use while teaching children in her church about health, and somehow Lauren ended up with it. Anita is one of those large, good-quality puppets that reminds me of the ones on *Sesame Street*, and Lauren used to communicate directly with her (as if she were a real person) as her "Nana" maneuvered the puppet's enormous mouth. Anita practically became a member of the family, especially when we were at the beach. She had a bathing suit and sunglasses, among many other outfits! We had some fun times and major belly-laughs over Anita, particularly when she cruised down the main strip of Myrtle Beach, performing her legendary "firecracker" cheer out of my mom's convertible ... and when Anita had a preplanned, very true-to-life wedding and reception one Saturday afternoon! (We all dressed up, and my husband was the minister!) We adults may have been a little crazy, but we all enjoyed being part of Lauren's imagina-tive world because it represented the love, joy, and innocence of one very special little girl.

One might think that with all the attention Lauren received, she would be a bit bratty; however, that wasn't the case at all. She was the sweetest, most unselfish child I've ever known. Many people told me stories of how Lauren had befriended kids at school who were teased by other kids, and she received the award for being the kindest student in her class every year. I never once saw Lauren talk back to anyone or pitch a fit, and the few times I saw her get called down were related to her desire for more candy! She was unusually obedient and respectful for a child of her age.

Lasting Impressions

After her death, I realized what an impact Lauren had made on those outside of our family as well. At the funeral home visitation, almost everyone commented about how sweet Lauren was and about how she was always smiling. When I returned to work, a coworker of mine (who didn't know Lauren) came up to me and said, "Mandy, I just want you to know that I've heard nothing but good things about that child." It means a lot to know that even in Lauren's short time on this earth, she made a significant and positive mark on it.

Lauren's personality was largely shaped by her Christian upbringing and her parents' great parental skills. However, I believe Lauren was who she was, primarily, because she was so full of love. My family has always had something very special and rare—a love and bond stronger than any I've ever known. Thanks to my silly "Papaw," we know how to have fun, too ... good, clean fun. In fact, the last thing Lauren had written on the board in her make-believe classroom was a promise that reflected the lessons she learned in our family: "I promise to ... Respect teachers, listen, be kind, help others, AND HAVE FUN!" I've always felt extremely blessed that God placed me into such a wonderful, loving family that taught me the values that are truly important in life; it's very comforting to know that Lauren enjoyed that same blessing as well.

Lauren was loved as much as any child could possibly be loved, and I believe that she, herself, extended and shared love and joy with others because of the abundant overflow of love that was poured into her. This concept testifies to the power of love and reminds me of a Scripture:

We love because he first loved us (1 John 4:19).

I believe if we truly feel loved by God the way He intends, then we can and should be vessels of love and joy, just like Lauren was.

Although she's no longer here with us, Lauren left me and countless others the gifts of her love and joy, and these gifts can live on in our hearts and in our actions forever. It's amazing how a young girl who lived only eleven short years on this earth has left such an outstanding legacy. Since I can't tell Lauren how proud I am of her for being such a sweet and loving person, the only way I know to honor and pay tribute to her is to share as much love and light as possible. So that's what I'll try to do. I ask that you help me keep Lauren's spirit alive here on earth by doing the same.

CHAPTER 17: CLOUDS WITH SILVER LININGS

Applied Faith

A s I illustrated in previous chapters, God's thoughts and ways are on a much higher level than ours; so it's very hard to make sense of why He allows tragedies, like Lauren's death, to occur. It's difficult to understand why God didn't answer the prayers and pleas of numerous people gathered at the hospital the night Lauren passed away. And it seems so unfair that my cousin, Lori (Lauren's mother), has lost her only beloved child when in her job as a child therapist, she daily counsels children who are abused or neglected by their parents. Naturally, our family has questioned God, "Why our Snuckums? Why us?!?" Random tragedies like this have always happened to *other* people, not to us. So we've been in uncharted waters, struggling to stay afloat.

A night or two after the accident, I remember sitting in my bed, crying uncontrollably and nearly drowning in sorrow. I was fearful that my family would never be happy again, and I started thinking about how many more losses I would likely have to face if I live a normal life expectancy. I quickly came to the conclusion that I couldn't allow myself to sit around and dwell on the sadness of this situation or the uncertainties of the future; otherwise, I would fall apart and be of no use to anyone—or even to God. So I decided to take a different approach and shift my focus away from my personal grief and toward the hope I have in God.

I reminded myself of the analogy of Wilbur at the vet and the themes I discussed in the chapter about God's tough love. I focused on the fact that God had His reasons for allowing this devastation to occur and that, somehow, He could bring good from it ... and I prayed that these purposes would be carried out according to His plan. In the darkest hours, I tried to shift the direction of my thoughts to the promises of Bible verses (some of which I've included in previous chapters), such as the following:

> I consider that our present sufferings are not worth comparing with the glory that will be revealed in us (Romans 8:18).

> And God will wipe away every tear from their eyes; there shall be no more death, nor sorrow, nor crying. There shall be no more pain, for the former things have passed away (Revelation 21:4, NKJV).

> Do not be anxious about anything, but in every situation, by prayer and petition, with thanksgiving, present your requests to God. And the peace of God, which transcends all understanding, will guard your hearts and your minds in Christ Jesus (Philippians 4:6-7).

> So we fix our eyes not on what is seen, but on what is unseen, since what is seen is temporary, but what is unseen is eternal (2 Corinthians 4:18).

Replacing my negative thoughts and feelings with encouraging verses from God's Word has worked wonders for me. This doesn't mean I'm living in a state of denial, but I'm intentionally putting my hope in Christ over my feelings. That doesn't mean that I always stop myself from crying when my emotions are stirred from a picture, a song, or a memory; I know I need time to grieve and mourn appropriately. But, as for dwelling on the sadness in my heart, I've decided not to do that. What good would that do me anyway?

I have learned some lessons and have grown spiritually and emotionally from this difficult experience. If I'm honest, I have to admit that I sure don't like some of the cold, hard facts I've come to know. For one thing, I've had to come to terms with the reality that my life on earth will sometimes be very difficult and painful. I don't want to be a negative person or to depress myself or anyone else, but I think it's necessary for me to prepare myself for the potentially long, hard journey ahead. Jesus, Himself, has assured us that "In this world you will have trouble" (John 16:33). But even as I prepare to encounter trials and heartaches, I know my focus must be on the latter half of John 16:33, which says, "But take heart! I have overcome the world." Jesus has made it possible for me to look at my life this way: I may have to endure many hardships in my years here on earth, but after that, I'll live happily ever after! And in light of eternity, spending even 100 years on earth is no more than the blink of an eye or a drop of water in the ocean.

Yes, Miss Lauren has taught me some valuable lessons. Because of her death, I've been able to discover the depth of my faith. I've had to cling to God and His promises more than ever before. Many times in these last months, those promises have been my only source of comfort. I've learned that I would have nothing without my faith in God; however, with my faith, there's nothing I can't do or get through. Despite the grief that my family and I have experienced, I'm closer to God than I've ever been. I'm now fully "convinced that neither death nor life, neither angels nor demons, neither the present nor the future, nor any powers, neither height nor depth, nor anything else in all creation, will be able to separate" me from God and the hope I have in Him (Romans 8:38-39).

⁕━━━⁘

The Bright Side

> Finally, brothers and sisters, whatever is true, whatever is noble, whatever is right, whatever is pure, whatever is lovely, whatever is admirable—if anything is excellent or praiseworthy— think about such things (Philippians 4:8).

How many of you habitually obey the verse above? If you're anything like me, your mind tends to venture toward negative, anxious thoughts instead; then you find yourself dwelling on those destructive thoughts. Even though I've improved in this area, I still struggle at times, especially now that my family and I have lost our bubbly little girl. (It's been a huge challenge trying not to worry about my grieving loved ones.) However, I've learned that it's during these difficult times when it's most crucial to obey Philippians 4:8. If I had not replaced my negative thoughts with a positive mindset, I don't know how I would've survived these past few months.

One of my very favorite Bible verses is 1 Corinthians 2:9, which states, "No eye has seen, no ear has heard, and no mind has imagined what God has prepared for those who love him" (NLT). I love this verse because it tells me that I, along with every other Christian, will experience joy in Heaven that far surpasses anything in my wildest dreams. Being married to a travel agent, I've been blessed to see many beautiful places. Once, in Ireland, I found myself moved to happy tears as I took in the view of lush green hillsides and majestic sea cliffs. I'm truly amazed by the beauty and diversity of God's creation here on earth, so I can't even begin to fathom how spectacular Heaven must be!

So I'm happy for Lauren, knowing that she's experiencing that beautiful place at this very moment. She is surrounded by perfection, feeling peace, joy, and pure love like never before. It's comforting to know that the sweet, innocent girl I love will never have to feel another ounce of physical pain or discomfort, the ache of rejection or a broken heart, or the intense grief of losing a loved one. In her eleven years, she never had to experience the death of a close loved one—not even a *great* grandparent or a pet—and now she never will. What a blessing for her!

According to her mom, Lauren's last day on earth was wonderful, spent playing at her house with a good friend. She then went to swim team practice that evening, and as she was swimming the lap right before the accident occurred, she stopped and looked up at her mom, smiling that big smile we all loved. One minute, Lauren was happy, doing one of her favorite things; the next, she was wrapped in heavenly arms, experiencing love and beauty that we can't even begin to imagine. So when I look at this event from Lauren's standpoint—"the bright side"—there are definitely some positive things to think about.

Loss Can Lead to Gain

Can you picture Heaven without children? I had never thought of it before Lauren's death, but I believe Heaven would be incomplete without them. We all know that children bring a special kind of joy and love into our lives, so it's understandable that God wants children surrounding Him throughout eternity. Scripture supports this idea because Jesus said:

> Let the little children come to me, and do not hinder them, for the kingdom of heaven belongs to such as these (Matt 19:14).

I know without a doubt that Lauren had to be one of the most precious children in the world, so she will bring God and all of those in

Heaven much love and joy. I've always believed that Heaven will be an amazing place; but now, knowing that I'll get to enjoy the company of a precious child who is so dear to my heart for all of eternity, I think it's going to be even better! We all wish Lauren was with us now, yet I choose to believe that our earthly loss will be our heavenly gain … There's no doubt that her childish presence will enhance the experiences of Heaven for her saved loved ones *forever*. I have a strong suspicion that Lauren will be among the first to welcome me and her other loved ones into Heaven when our times come. I can picture her with wide eyes and a big smile on her face, bouncing enthusiastically to my side and then taking my hand to guide me, saying, "Mandy, you've GOT to see this place!"

I truly believe that Lauren's death will lead others to life—both here and eternally. "Lauren's Fund" has been established in memory and honor of her, and quite a large sum of money has already been raised to go toward a worthy cause. This money may help ensure that metal ladders in swimming pools are replaced with ones made of fiberglass or that needy children will be assisted, thus saving or enhancing the lives of children here on earth in memory of Lauren.[6] More than that, my prayer is that any unsaved person who loved Lauren will want the assurance of seeing her again one day and will seek to know Jesus so they can. If her death leads even one soul to Christ, I know Lauren's joy will be even more complete.

The sudden, tragic loss of Lauren's life reminds us of how important it is to live life to the fullest and to love in ways we will never regret. The news of Lauren's death traveled nationally, and I imagine that many people hugged their loved ones a little longer and tighter after they heard about her story. My family is now more aware of how fragile each

---

[6] If you would like to make a contribution to Lauren's Fund, you can do the following: 1) Send checks made payable to Lauren Cecil Scholarship Fund to 7182 NC Hwy 8, Lexington, NC 27292 2) Paypal: www.paypal.com, click "Send Money," enter laurensfund@gmail.com and the amount, click "Send Money to Friends" 3) Drop off cash or transfer funds at any New Bridge Bank location. Send comments and questions to LaurensFund@gmail.com

one of our lives is, and I believe that through our loss, we have gained an even greater appreciation for one another than we had before. We have learned that priorities and perceptions change when we're faced with the harsh reality that none of us is guaranteed another breath. My husband is a great example of our new priorities. After Lauren's death, he *finally* mustered up the courage to make a job change, allowing him to have more time for the important things in life.

Also, as a result of Lauren's death, families, friends, churches, and the community at large have come together like I've never witnessed before. The outpouring of love, prayers, and support has been unbelievable. The day following Lauren's funeral, family and friends gathered to plant a memory garden next to Lauren's swing set in her honor. I believe many of us have bonded during this difficult time, and I've been blessed to feel the love and support of many people. So, although much has surely been lost because of Lauren's tragic death, I believe many things have been gained as well. To tie this theme into a Wilbur analogy, I believe God has given (and will continue to give) me and all of Lauren's loved ones some "carrots" of consolation for our devastating loss.

<hr />

Rainbows and Butterflies

I have received numerous God-given signs throughout my life, and since Lauren's death, God has displayed some remarkable signs to me and many others. For example, an upside-down rainbow, which looked like a smiley face, appeared in the sky above the pool right after Lauren died. Similarly, I saw a smiley face imprinted in my powder makeup compact the following Sunday as I was getting ready for church. Several nights after Lauren passed away, her parents prayed for a sign, and God gave them one the very next morning in the form of a miraculous phone call. But an extra-special sign was revealed to my family and me as we were on our annual family beach trip about a month after Lauren passed away.

Wanting to do something special to remember Lauren, several of us ordered 20 live butterflies to release during our beach trip; they were to be shipped overnight to our rented beach house for the day of release. When we arrived at the beach, many of my family members gathered on the front porch, discussing the various visions and signs that several people had been given in the weeks following Lauren's death. Her parents said they had been longing and praying for God to give them visions or special dreams of Lauren—anything that would allow them to feel a connection to her. So, knowing that the butterflies would be arriving in a few days, I began praying diligently that God would give us all an obvious sign through the butterfly release. I had no doubt that God could do it; the only question was whether or not He would.

When the time came to release the butterflies, my family gathered by the pool in the back yard of the beach house. My husband began by reading a poem I had written about Lauren. I said a silent prayer as her parents then opened the lid of the box that contained the butterflies. The experience of watching those delicate little creatures begin to flap their wings and fly was breathtaking. After all of the butterflies had flown from the box, we noticed that one had landed on Lauren's mother, Lori, and that one was on me as well. At this discovery, I suspected that God was getting ready to show off! Time seemed to stand still. One minute ... two minutes ... nearly five minutes passed, and the precious creatures remained attached to our clothing—one near my right hip and one on the center of Lori's stomach. I was in awe, practically speechless, and I don't think there was a dry eye among us.

I looked down at the light brown butterfly on my hip as it looked up at me with its tiny eyes and said, "Hello, little one!" And when I gently waved at it with my hand, it flew away. I looked over at Lori, Lauren's mother, and was happy to see that "her" butterfly was still there. (It was a vibrant orange color, noticeably prettier than all the other light brown ones.) I was beginning to wonder if the butterfly would ever leave. Finally it crawled upward, toward Lori's heart, and then fluttered off. Instead of flying up in the air, though, it flew down and landed on Lauren's father's leg for a brief moment before it touched down on the ground. It appeared to struggle for a moment, but then it suddenly darted into the air, flying much faster and higher than any butterfly I'd ever seen—looking more like a miniature missile than a butterfly! In an instant, the butterfly was so high that it disappeared into the evening sky.

As we watched the butterfly disappear, we were awed by the symbolism of its flight ... This was our extraordinary sign from above. Butterflies are symbolic of new life, and I felt as if God allowed Lauren to be represented by them, particularly by the beautiful orange one that lingered on her mother. I interpreted the sign to mean that God had allowed us to be blessed by Lauren's lovely presence for a little while and that she enjoyed being among us. But she abruptly had to say goodbye in order to fulfill a higher calling. I believe this symbolism implies that we must accept the fact that Lauren was able to stay with us for only a brief time and understand that God has her exactly where she now belongs. We must be grateful for the special time we had with her and for the wonderful impact she made on our lives. And we must also believe that even though she has disappeared from our sight, she is happier and freer than ever before.

My family and I are very thankful for this obvious sign from God. It's a confirmation that Lauren is in His loving arms. It's also confirmation that God sees our grief and wants to comfort us. This amazing sign is yet another positive, praiseworthy thing for me to think about when I'm tempted to cave in to my sadness. I want you to be encouraged by the things I've shared regarding this tragic loss in my life, believing that you, too, can find goodness and blessings in the midst of the storms in your life if you keep your mind on things above. Praise God, there's absolutely NO cloud that cannot be traced with a silver lining when our hope and trust is in Him!

A Poem for Lauren

I can't help but believe that God had a change of heart,
For it seemed you were an angel right from the very start.
So He placed you in a special cocoon, wrapped in layer upon layer of love,
Until the time suddenly came to take you up above.
Then He whispered sweetly in your ear, "Now spread your wings and fly,
My little angelic butterfly!"

CONCLUSION: THE END OF THE TAIL

> The Son is the image of the invisible God, the firstborn
> over all creation. For in him all things were created:
> things in heaven and on earth, visible and invisible ...
> all things have been created through him and for him
> (Colossians 1:15-16).

I believe God made dogs for one major purpose: to bring us joy. Their lives do not have comparable value to human lives, but they aren't "*just* dogs," as some people believe. They have distinct personalities and unique ways of sharing love and joy. Dogs seem to have been instilled with some of the extraordinary qualities of God ... They give unconditional love, easily forgive and forget, and are exceptionally loyal. Dogs stay by our sides through the good times and the bad, enhancing our lives in so many different ways. They can teach us some valuable lessons, too.

God has used a mischievous little dachshund to steal my heart and teach me many things about Himself, myself, and life in general. I have discovered that Wilbur and I have a lot in common, and I've learned that I should actually aspire to be more like him in many ways. Through my experiences with Wilbur, I've gained invaluable insights pertaining to my sinful, disobedient nature and God's amazing love and grace. By attempting to see things through Wilbur's eyes, I'm better able to grasp the fact that I know and understand only a tiny, miniscule fraction of what my Master does. I also have more respect for God, understanding that even though I don't always think His ways are best for me, they always are. I know that if I will stay close by my Master's side and trust Him through the storms in my life, He will eventually work everything out for my good.

Since this book has revolved around analogies, I want to conclude it with one more—one which I believe encompasses every theme I've discussed and illustrates the central theme of Christianity ...

The evening before Lauren's death, my husband, Wilbur, and I were walking home from my grandparents' house. Suddenly, we encountered a large copperhead snake near our mailbox! Since it was almost dark outside, we didn't see it until we were about a foot from it. Had I not jerked Wilbur away, he would've gotten right up in its face. I was terrified! I don't think it's possible to meet a person who is more scared of snakes than me—I can't even look at a picture of one without squealing! Although I had never seen a snake in our yard before, this was certainly the real deal. Initially, I was too shocked to scream or cry; I just darted into the house. But once everything registered in my mind, I was a mess, crying and demanding that my husband kill the snake!

My husband was pretty scared, too, and refused to go after the snake with a hoe, fearing that if he swung and missed, it would strike him. Instead, he got in his car, planning to run over it. This didn't seem like a good solution to me because I felt sure the snake would slither away before he got the chance to kill it. I was right, the snake got away ... which meant there was a huge, poisonous snake somewhere in our yard!!!

I immediately got on the phone and called my grandma, aunt, and mom—three people I knew would empathize with me in my hysterical state (they are also terrified of snakes). I even posted the story on Facebook, requesting prayer, and became so irrational that I made my husband search every square inch of our house for any snakes! I kept thinking about how differently this scenario could have played out; had he been bitten, Wilbur most likely would've died from the snake's poisonous venom. This reality hit me hard, and I silently thanked God that all of us were okay. It took a while for me to settle down after this ordeal. There was so much adrenaline pumping through me that I didn't fall asleep that night until after 3:00 a.m.

The tragedy involving Lauren occurred the following evening, so I didn't give much more thought to the snake encounter until a friend mentioned it to me at the funeral home visitation. She had seen my post about the snake on Facebook and insinuated that she believed the snake may have been an impending omen of Lauren's death. I still didn't give much thought to the snake confrontation or the possible irony of it until about a week later. As I was about to pull into my driveway after visiting with Lauren's parents, the snake incident came to my mind, and I felt God speaking to my spirit. I became aware of the symbolism that surrounded the snake encounter, and goose bumps appeared on my arms.

Before I explain what God shared with me, I need to fill you in about a few things. You see, we have a flagpole extending from a utility pole in our front yard, several feet behind our mailbox. I had been asking my husband to change the decorative flag for several weeks before the snake incident took place because it was July, and we still had our Easter flag hanging! This was really starting to bother and embarrass me. The pastel-colored flag, featuring a cross and frilly, floral designs, was obviously meant to be displayed at Easter or in the spring—not in the heat of summer. I had repeatedly asked my husband to put up our patriotic July 4th flag, but he had not done so. As it turns out, I'm happy he *didn't* fulfill my request because God used our Easter flag to give me an awesome sign. You see, when the snake slithered off that evening, it went directly beneath the flag in our front yard. Do you see the symbolism in that?

I know it wasn't coincidence that the first and only time I had ever seen a snake in our yard was the evening before the darkest day of my life. The incident served as the perfect metaphor. The snake, which is an iconic symbol of evil, came upon us suddenly and out of nowhere, just as Lauren's death did. The copperhead snake is no joke—it's poisonous and lethal, and from an earthly standpoint, so is death. Death is horrible and hopeless in the natural realm; the finality of it cuts deep. It can seem impossible to get over the death of a loved one, especially when that loved one is a child who was so full of love and life. But with God it's possible to be happy again, to live again. Jesus conquered death, and I know this is what God clearly illustrated to me through the symbolism of our cross flag towering over that snake.

I was about to turn into my driveway the moment God gave me this insight and message. When I came within viewing distance of the flag, I studied it closely because I knew something was written on it, but I had forgotten what it was. After I saw the words on the flag, I was filled with emotion and began to cry happy tears ... The message read: "REJOICE! HE IS ALIVE!"

It amazes me that in my time of sorrow, God turned the scary snake encounter into a sign of hope. He used it to demonstrate the fundamental message of Christianity, the key point I want you to take from this book. That message is this: **GOD WINS!**

Yes, the evil serpent got away and is roaming freely on this earth, and it's unnerving to live with that presence nearby. The devil is dangerous and deadly, intent on destroying everyone and everything he possibly can. He has done a fine job of leading many people astray (including me at times) and wreaking havoc upon our fallen world. Crimes, terrorism, wars, sex trafficking, deadly diseases, and catastrophic natural disasters are just a few of the terrible things that will continue for an appointed time. As a result of sin, all of us will experience the heartaches and pains of this life for our allotted times. But praise God, the devil won't get the final say! GOD will reign forever and ever and ever! Christ is triumphant; His tomb is empty! "'Death has been swallowed up in victory'" (1 Corinthians 15:54). So if you belong to Him, you need to rejoice! No matter what your current circumstances may be, you can share and celebrate in Christ's victory, knowing that you are on the way to a place where no more storm clouds can rise ... a place where you will live and reign with God and His people in love, joy, and peace throughout eternity!!!

I pray that you have been encouraged and that your faith has been strengthened by the messages I've shared in this book. I hope you have enjoyed reading about my "Wilbur analogies" and the lessons I've learned from my best four-legged friend ... the lessons that have brought me closer to God. It's my prayer that you are thoroughly convinced that God loves you and wants to have a genuine relationship with you. Above all, I hope you have accepted Christ's gift of eternal life. For those of you who have trusted Jesus to be your Lord and Savior, I pray you will walk close by His side, faithfully loving Him and staying loyal to His cause. Always remember that with Jesus as your Master, you have the assurance of being loved, protected, and guided throughout your life, and you will be rewarded with an abundance of *everlasting* treats!

> Then I heard *every creature* in heaven and on earth and under the earth and on the sea, and all that is in them, saying: **"To him who sits on the throne and to the Lamb be praise and honor and glory and power, for ever and ever!"** (Revelation 5:13, emphasis mine). **AMEN!**

Acknowledgements

I want to give a very special thanks to my husband, Shane ...

Thanks for faithfully loving and supporting me over the past nine years. You have been my number one fan, always encouraging me and cheering me on to become the woman God wants me to be. Your hard work and support have made it possible for me to complete this book, and I'm so grateful to you. You're definitely one of a kind, and I'm truly blessed to be loved by you and to have you as my husband. I love you!

I want to say a special thank you to my Daddy, Mama, Stepdad, Granny, Papaw, and other close family members; and to my "second mother," Brenda, and my lifelong best friend, Maria ...

Thank you all so much for your love, guidance, and support. You have each made a huge impact on my life and nurtured my walk with God. I'm abundantly blessed and extremely grateful to have you in my life. All of you hold a very special place in my heart. I love you!

I also want to give thanks to my editor, Carrie B. McWhorter ...

I am so thankful that God allowed us to meet at the Blue Ridge Mountains Christian Writers Conference in 2012. I thought you would be a great editor, and you certainly didn't prove me wrong! Thank you for all of your dedication, work, and literary expertise. This journey has been a challenge for me, to say the least, and I don't know what I would've done without you. Thank you so much!

Last, but certainly not least, I want to thank God ...

According to the medical experts, I was never supposed to be born, so I want to thank You for giving me life. Thank You for placing me into such a wonderful family and for blessing me with an amazing husband and many special friends. I also thank You for Wilbur, who has brought much love and joy into my life and inspired me to write this book.

Lord, I'm also grateful to You for allowing me to live in such a privileged country and for blessing me with shelter, food, and many material comforts that I too often take for granted. Most importantly, thank You for the sacrifices You made to save me. You are my Savior, my Lord, and my Best Friend, and I'm so grateful for Your unconditional love and forgiveness. You are truly awesome, and there is no way I can ever glorify or praise You enough! I love you!

Love,
Mandy

Mandy, age 3, with her best buddy, Heidi

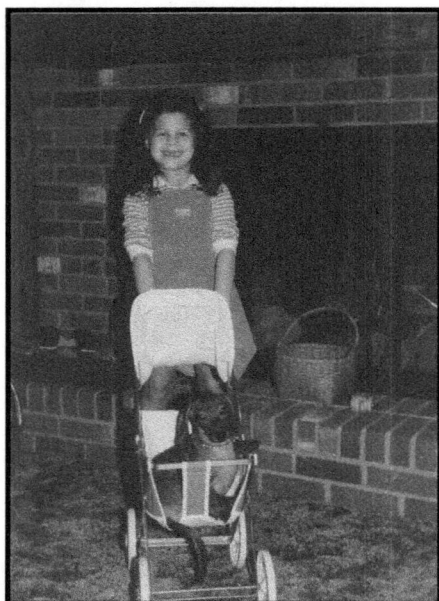

Mandy, age 7, and her "baby," Bridgett

Mandy, age 9, with her "siblings," Bridgett and Abby

Growing up together: Bridgett, Abby (in background), and Mandy, age 15

Abby (left) and Bridgett (right) in their later years

Little Winnie, 2003

Baby Wilbur, 2007

Young Wilbur, so full of personality!

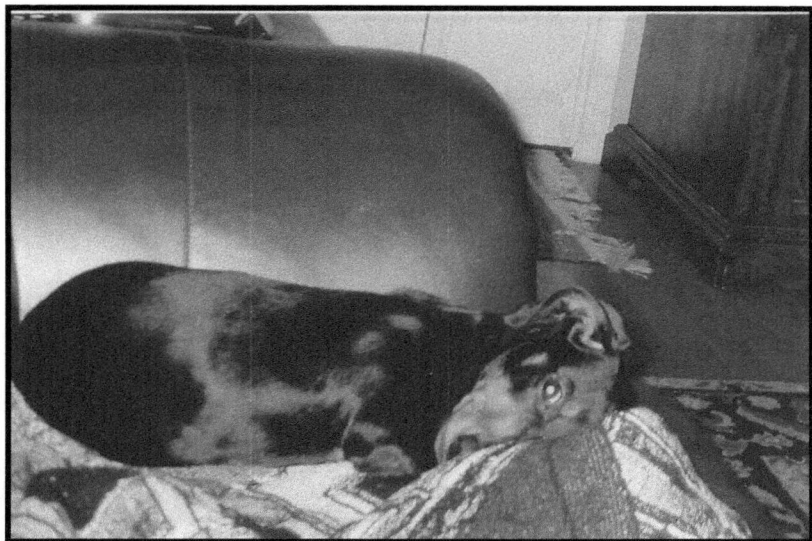

"Yes, I know I'm adorable!"

"Please give me some of that pizza!"

Mandy enjoying some sweet Wilbur kisses

Mandy, Shane, and "Reindeer" Wilbur, Christmas 2012

Wilbur and Lauren, October 2012

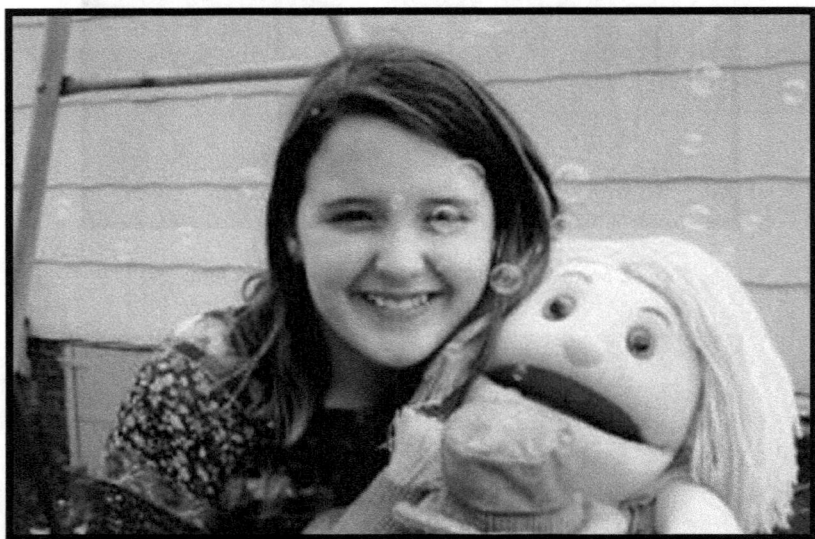

Blowing bubbles: Lauren and her puppet, "Anita"

Lauren and her "baby," C.C., at Lauren's 11th birthday party, May 2013

Mandy's family (Lauren, center) at the 100th
annual Conrad family reunion in 2012

www.ingramcontent.com/pod-product-compliance
Lightning Source LLC
Chambersburg PA
CBHW071532040426
42452CB00008B/986